WITHDRAWN
HARVARD LIBRARY
WITHDRAWN

God of Mercy
Ælfric's Sermons and Theology

Ælfric, Abbot of Eynsham.

God of Mercy
Ælfric's Sermons and Theology

translated and introduced by
Carmen Acevedo Butcher

MERCER
UNIVERSITY PRESS

ISBN 0-86554-994-X   MUP/P328

God of Mercy: Ælfric's Sermons and Theology
©2006 Mercer University Press
1400 Coleman Avenue
Macon, Georgia 31207 USA
All rights reserved
Printed in the United States of America

First edition, March 2006

The paper used in this publication meets the minimum
requirements of American National Standard for Information
Sciences—Permanence of Paper for Printed Library Materials,
ANSI Z39.48-1984.

Library of Congress Cataloging-in-Publication Data

[CIP is available from the Library of Congress.]

Contents

Preface ix

Acknowledgments xi

Introduction 1

Sermons
   I. For the Nativity of the Lord (Christmas).
      John 1.1-14. 27
   II. For the Sixth Day [Friday] in the First Week of Lent.
      John 5.1-15. 39
   III. For the Sixth Day [Friday] in the Second Week of Lent.
      Matthew 21.33-46. 48
   IV. For the Third Sunday in Lent.
      Luke 11.14-28; Matthew 12.22-30. 53
   V. For the Sixth Day [Friday] in the Third Week of Lent.
      John 4.5-42. 61
   VI. For the Sixth Day [Friday] in the Fourth Week of Lent.
      John 11.1-45. 69
   VII. For the Fourth Sunday after Easter.
      John 16.5-14. 77
   VIII. For the Fifth Sunday after Easter.
      John 16.23-30. 84
   IX. For the Sunday after the Ascension of the Lord.
      John 15.26-16.4. 90
   X. For Pentecost Sunday.
      John 14.23-31. 96
   XI. Sermon to the People,
      Delivered on the Octave of Pentecost. 101
   XII. For the First Sunday after Pentecost.
      John 3.1-15. 113
   XIII. For the Fifth Sunday after Pentecost.
      Luke 6.36-42. 119
   XIV. For the Sixth Sunday after Pentecost.
      Luke 5.1-11. 125
   XV. For the Seventh Sunday after Pentecost.
      Matthew 5.20-24. 131

XVI. For the Tenth Sunday after Pentecost.
   Luke 16.1-9. 138
XVII. For the Twelfth Sunday after Pentecost.
   Mark 7.31-37. 145

Selected Bibliography
   Works Used for the Translations in This Volume 153
   Editions of Works by Ælfric 153
   Reference Sources 154
   Primary Sources 156
   Secondary Sources 157

The love that loves God is not idle. Instead, it is strong and works great things always. And if love isn't willing to work, then it isn't love. God's love must be seen in the actions of our mouths and minds and bodies. A person must fulfill God's word with goodness.
—Ælfric, "For Pentecost Sunday"

And we ought to worship with true humility if we want our heavenly God to hear us because God is the one who lives in a high place and yet has regard for the deep down humble, and God is always near to those who sincerely call to him in their trouble. . . . Without humility no person can thrive in the Lord.
—Ælfric, "For the Sixth Day [Friday]
in the Third Week of Lent";
"For the First Sunday after Pentecost"

Bosses who cannot permit those working under them to know kindness during this life of labor should never themselves enjoy lives of luxury because they could easily be kind to their workers every day. And then they would have some kindness in their souls. God loves kindness.
—Ælfric, "For the Fifth Sunday after Pentecost"

For Sean, Kate, John

Preface

Ælfric lived a millennium ago, but his manuscripts describe a God of mercy as contemporary as the twenty-first century. He defines *love* as a verb, *obedience* as joy, and *humility* and *kindness* as synonyms.[1] The person reading his work joins a vibrant, ancient, eclectic community.[2] Seventeen of Ælfric's best sermons are translated here, each introduced by a brief discussion of its relevant historical context, medieval themes, numerology, typology, and stylistic matters. Bracketed asterisks ([* * *]) in sermons I and XVII indicate lacunae in their source, the Old English manuscript Cotton Vitellius C.v., and are explained in the introductions to these bookend sermons.

Translations from Old English and Latin are my own. A general introduction frames these sermons by outlining the monastic context of Ælfric's work, the immensity of his corpus and its *Rule of St. Benedict* center, his theological concerns and humane style (as contrasted with Archbishop Wulfstan's trenchant pulpiteering), and my translation philosophy.

---

[1] This statement refers to *God of Mercy*'s opening quotations. See John C. Pope, *Homilies of Ælfric: A Supplementary Collection. Being Twenty-One Full Homilies of His Middle and Later Career for the Most Part Not Previously Edited, with Some Shorter Pieces, Mainly Passages Added to the Second and Third Series*, 2 vols., Early English Text Society (EETS) 259, 260 (London: Oxford University Press, 1967, 1968) I.398-99 (X.59-64), I.296 (V.180-84), II.499-500 (XIII.62-67a), and I.486 (XII.172). References to Ælfric's sermons follow the roman numerals in Pope. Citations to Pope's *Homilies* give roman volume number and Arabic page number(s) separated by a period, followed by the parenthetic roman sermon number and Arabic line number(s) separated by a period.

[2] Elizabeth Elstob (1683–1756) and other early Saxonists studied Ælfric because they were fascinated with the Old English language and also because they felt his sermons supported Anglican doctrine. In 1709 Elstob published the first critical edition of a sermon by Ælfric, *An English-Saxon Homily on the Birth-day of St. Gregory: Anciently Used in the English-Saxon Church. Giving an account of the conversion of the English from paganism to Christianity, Translated into Modern English, with Notes, Etc.* (London: W. Bowyer). In its preface Elstob defends the study of Old English: "[Understanding] the Faith, Religion, the Laws and Customs, and Language of . . . [our] . . . Ancestors . . . are Considerations which have afforded me no small Encouragement in the Prosecution of these Studies" (vi). This preface, the sermon facsimile, introduction, bibliography, and other critical apparatus can be read online at the Elizabeth Elstob website created by Timothy Graham, designed by John Chandler, and sponsored by The Medieval Institute, Western Michigan University, and the Department of Special Collections, Hesburgh Library, University of Notre Dame (Kalamazoo MI: Board of the Medieval Institute, 2002) <http://www.wmich.edu/medieval/research/rawl/elstob/cover.html> (cited 11 October 2004).

Acknowledgments

This book began during a Fulbright at University College London (UCL) and was completed during a Fulbright lectureship at Sogang University in Seoul. The first grant enabled research engaging the meticulous 1967–1968 Old English edition of these sermons by John C. Pope, which I discussed in my article, "Recovering Unique Ælfrician Texts Using the Fiber Optic Light Cord (FOLC)," in *Old English Newsletter* (2003). Bruce Mitchell of Oxford's St. Edmund Hall, the late R. I. Page of the Parker Library in Cambridge, and the late John Dodgson of UCL made the British research rewarding, while Horace Underwood, Jai-Ok Shim (past and present executive directors of the Korean-American Educational Commission), Chair Sook-Whan Cho, and the entire cosmopolitan Sogang Humanities Department made a city of eleven million seem cozy.

Without John Algeo's sagacity, this book would not have been. *Magnae gratiae.* Jonathan Evans, Rosemary Franklin, Walter Gordon, and the late William Provost of the University of Georgia (UGA) suggested excellent early revisions. Harold Newman, William Rice, and David Fillingim receive special thanks for their Shorter College support. Expert librarians who make research possible deserve golden credit: Kim Herndon, Bettie Sumner, DeWayne Williams, and John Rivest at Shorter, as well as those at UGA, Senate House, the British Library, Oxbridge colleges, and Sogang's Loyola Library. And Edmon L. Rowell, Jr., senior editor at Mercer University Press, carefully read the manuscript, improving it immeasurably with his astute suggestions. Even with this fine help, every error remains my responsibility.

The sisters and brothers of the Order of St. Benedict have provided friendship and a true lifeline to Ælfric's spirit. Loren and Doris Acevedo gave the brightest grandparental aid. Above all, the British wit and kindness of Sean Butcher and the joie de vivre of Kate and John kept this book alive.

Carmen Acevedo Butcher

Introduction
An Anglo-Saxon Benedictine Monk

The late tenth- and early eleventh-century sermons translated here for the first time into Modern English represent the best earliest English sermons surviving into the third millennium. Conceived in the discipline Benedictines know, they were written by a conscientious monk who left careful instructions to future scribes to copy his works carefully because he did not want their scholarly, salvation-bringing words marred by the introduction of unorthodox passages and scribal errors. Through the centuries, however, Ælfric's sermons were threatened by the terrorism of Viking axes and the dangerous banality of human neglect when—some seven hundred years after their composition—they nearly perished in the Cotton Fire of 1731 that scorched or destroyed almost 1,000 invaluable ancient works.

Ælfric was a Benedictine monk born around AD 950.[1] He spent his days in a humble habit, rising, sleeping, eating, and writing on the monastery timetables, his soul centered on Psalms singing. *God of Mercy*'s seventeen brief sermons reflect this focus. The *Opus Dei* was Ælfric's life, and he sang God's praises as much as or more than he wrote of them. It is safe to say Ælfric practiced what he preached.

We see him hunched over many a folio of vellum, stylus in hand, looking like any other monk, but Ælfric has been named the greatest, most prolific prose writer of the Anglo-Saxon period, and the greatest teacher after the Venerable Bede,[2] though scant documentation of his accomplished

---

[1]The dating of Ælfric's life cannot be exact. Malcolm Godden convincingly argues "around 950," which strikes an amicable balance between the various points of view. See his *Ælfric's Catholic Homilies: Introduction, Commentary, and Glossary*, EETS (Oxford: Oxford University Press, 2001) xxi, xxix-xxxii; hereafter shortened to *Introduction, Commentary, and Glossary*. Compare Peter Clemoes, "The Chronology of Ælfric's Works," in *The Anglo-Saxons*, ed. Clemoes, 212-47. For the claim that a first-person passage included by Ælfric in his medieval grammar book suggests an earlier date for his birth, a notion Godden refutes, see Jonathan Wilcox, *Ælfric's Prefaces*, Durham Medieval Texts 9 (Durham: Durham Medieval Texts, 1994) 7. There is very little documentation to support any birth date without qualification.

[2]The voices praising Ælfric are many. R. W. Chambers eloquently argues for the monk's seminal influence on English prose, noting that Ælfric's "cultured prose" continued to be copied even after the Norman Conquest. See *On the Continuity of English Prose from Alfred to More and His School*, EETS OS 186a, 1932 (London: Oxford University Press, 1950) lxi, xc, xciii. Peter Clemoes says "Ælfric's prose can be judged by the standards of all time" and points out it is "very early in the European tradition for there to be a vernacular prose of such scope and quality as Ælfric's" and "several centuries were to pass before it was matched in English prose again." For an outstanding analysis of Ælfric's achievements as

life remains. Because only two dates can be determined with certainty, Ælfric's biography has an anonymity appropriate for a Benedictine monk who preferred the advancement of God's kingdom over human accolades. This personal obscurity is also synonymous with his main message: Christ should become more visible as his followers become humbler, kinder (and less obvious), for this is the way to follow a loving, forgiving God. In every one of his sermons, Ælfric preaches the God of mercy.

Ælfric's Writing as Integral to His Monkhood

Ælfric spent his formative years in the rich Benedictine Reformation environment at Winchester, under the mentoring of Bishop Æthelwold (AD

---

a writer, see Clemoes, "Ælfric," in *Continuations and Beginnings: Studies in Old English Literature*, ed. Stanley (London: Thomas Nelson and Sons, Ltd., 1966) 178, 206. Milton McC. Gatch calls Ælfric "the most important theological figure of the late Anglo-Saxon church" and "the greatest prose stylist of the Old English period." See Gatch, *Preaching and Theology in Anglo-Saxon England: Ælfric and Wulfstan* (Toronto: University of Toronto Press, 1977) 12. Like Clemoes, Gatch maintains the monk's prodigious production of vernacular preaching texts is a unique accomplishment—in no other language were vernacular sermons written in a volume comparable to that in Old English before the end of the eleventh century, and of this distinguished group, Ælfric stands apart. See Gatch, "The Achievement of Ælfric and His Colleagues in European Perspective" in *The Old English Homily and Its Backgrounds*, ed. Szarmach and Huppé (Albany: State University of New York Press, 1978) 43-73. David M. Knowles identifies Ælfric as "one of the most distinguished figures in the history of Western theological learning" of his time and "second only to Bede" as a theologian and teacher. See *The Monastic Order in England*, 2nd ed. (Cambridge: Cambridge University Press, 1963) 63. Sir Frank Merry Stenton describes this monk as "the greatest insular scholar of the Benedictine reformation" and his *Catholic Homilies* as "the classic example of Anglo-Saxon prose." See Stenton's enduring *Anglo-Saxon England*, 3rd ed. (Oxford: Oxford University Press, 2001) 343, 396. Eugene A. Green believes Ælfric's homilies "left a record of Christian education during the tenth and eleventh centuries that outdistances the efforts of anyone else for centuries on either side of his life." See "Ælfric the Catechist" in *De Ore Domini: Preacher and Word in the Middle Ages*, SMC XXVII, ed. Amos, Green, and Kienzle (Kalamazoo: Medieval Institute Publications, 1989) 62. Jonathan Wilcox judges Ælfric "the most important homilist and most prolific writer of Old English" and notes that "[a]rtful and efficient prose is a hallmark of Ælfric's writing." See *Ælfric's Prefaces*, 1, 56. Wilcox's introduction focuses on the implications of Ælfric's believing his corpus in Old English provides an authoritative body of doctrine, a unique claim for vernacular writing at such an early period. Robert Boenig describes Ælfric as "the literary giant of the later Anglo-Saxon era." See *Anglo-Saxon Spirituality: Selected Writings*, Classics of Western Spirituality (New York: Paulist Press, 2000) 49; 28, 46. This handful of scholars' comments on Ælfric's importance is merely representative.

963–984). Five years after being ordained a deacon, Ælfric became a priest at the canonical age of thirty. We know with certainty that in 987 Bishop Ælfheah sent Ælfric to the southwest of England, to a new monastery in Cernel.³ Known today as Cerne Abbas, this village is a popular destination—not for Ælfric's Anglo-Saxon abbey ruins—but for tourists seeking the 180-foot chalk figure of a club-brandishing naked man, cut into the hillside perhaps in pre-Saxon times. Here among Cernel's gentle green hills, Ælfric began (or, as some scholars suggest, continued) his writing career more than a millennium ago.⁴ The year 1005 is his other documented biographical date.⁵ Ælfric left Cernel that year at the age of perhaps fifty-five for nobleman Æthelmær's new monastery in Eynsham, a long eighty-five-mile journey inland in the direction of Oxford. Here he lived out his life as Eynsham's first abbot, from 1005 until his death, around 1014.⁶

---

³G. I., Needham, ed., *Ælfric: Lives of Three English Saints*, Exeter Medieval English Texts, M. J. Swanton, gen. ed., 2nd ed., 1966 (Exeter: University of Exeter, 1984) 15; P. H. Sawyer, *Anglo-Saxon Charters: An Annotated List and Bibliography* (London: Butler & Tanner, Ltd., 1968) 356, Stenton, *Anglo-Saxon England*, 458-60; and Donald Matthew, *Atlas of Medieval Europe* (Oxford: Phaidon Press, Ltd., 1986) 48. For information on Cerne Abbas, see David M. Knowles, *Bare Ruined Choirs: The Dissolution of the English Monasteries* (Cambridge: Cambridge University Press, 1976) 239 and David M. Knowles and R. Neville Hadcock, *Medieval Religious Houses: England and Wales* (London: Longman Group, Ltd., 1971) 53, 62.

⁴Godden suggests Ælfric may have begun writing after he finished his education at Winchester (ca. 967–ca. 977); he also hypothesizes these "lost years" of Ælfric (ca. 967/977–987) may have found him writing Latin sermons for Winchester monks, clerics, and students, providing a starting point for his later vernacular work. See *Introduction, Commentary, and Glossary*, xxxi; xxi. For more information on the Cerne Abbas Giant, see Rodney Legg, *Cerne's Giant and Village Guide* (Sherborne: Dorset Publishing Co., 1986) 4-15.

⁵F. E. Harmer, *Anglo-Saxon Writs* (Manchester: Manchester University Press, 1952) 8; A. J. Robertson, *Anglo-Saxon Charters* (Cambridge: Cambridge University Press, 1939) 386, 465; H. E. Salter, ed., *Eynsham Cartulary*, 2 vols., Oxford Historical Society 49, 51 (Oxford: Clarendon Press, 1907, 1908) I.vii.; Sawyer, *Anglo-Saxon Charters*, 278; Stenton, *Anglo-Saxon England*, 458-60. For more information on Eynsham, see Knowles and Hadcock, *Medieval Religious Houses*, 54, 65; A. Hardy, A. Dodd, and G. D. Keevil, eds., *Ælfric's Abbey: Excavations at Eynsham Abbey, Oxfordshire, 1989–1992*, Thames Valley Landscapes Monograph 15 (Oxford: Oxbow Books Limited, 2002); John Godfrey, *The Church in Anglo-Saxon England* (Cambridge: Cambridge University Press, 1962) 333. At latitude 51.48 N and longitude 1.22 W, Medieval Eynsham was five miles northwest of present-day Oxford. See David Hill, *An Atlas of Anglo-Saxon England* (Oxford: Basil Blackwell, 1981) 151, 157-58.

⁶Dorothy Whitelock chooses this approximate death date. See "Two Notes on Ælfric and Wulfstan," in *History, Law and Literature in 10th–11th Century England*, 1943

Ælfric's writing career lasted some twenty-five to fifty years. His method of composition was to consult and draw on the works of the established church fathers particularly in three homiletic anthologies by Paul the Deacon, Smaragdus, and Haymo, and he did so with a sinewy memory much exercised by his monastic calling.[7] Ælfric did not write in a vacuum. He saw himself as a monk in a long line of writers transmitting a heritage of Latin patristic learning, and he was determined to discharge his obligation in a fastidious, scholarly fashion, resulting in sermons that are, according to Jonathan Wilcox, "deliberatively derivative." However, like any good writer, Ælfric shaped his sources and developed his own style.[8] Paul E. Szarmach points out that "however sane, sober, and clear literary historians paint" Ælfric the writer, he "had a restless streak in him. . . . For Ælfric, composition was a process, not an event." That restlessness of a great writer notwithstanding, this Anglo-Saxon Benedictine monk wrote year after year as a way to serve the Church and preserve his own salvation. This is how he fulfilled his responsibilities to the Truth, whom he believed was "that true Light, our Savior Christ, who enlightened all the world."[9]

The Catholic Homilies and Their Audience

Glorifying this Truth is Ælfric's clear pedagogical purpose in his most important work; the eighty sermons of the two-volume *Catholic Homilies* (989, 992) provide a solid foundation for the Christocentric educational plan he worked on during his monastic life.[10] Here for the first time in the

---

(London: Variorum Reprints, 1981) 122-26. Compare Boenig, *Anglo-Saxon Spirituality*, 16.

[7]Pope, *Homilies* I.154-56. Compare Wilcox, *Ælfric's Prefaces*, 23.

[8]Wilcox, *Ælfric's Prefaces*, 23. For a good discussion of Ælfric's rhythmical prose, see Pope, *Homilies* I.105ff.

[9]Paul E. Szarmach, "Ælfric Revises: The Lives of Martin and the Idea of the Author" in *Unlocking the Wordhord: Anglo-Saxon Studies in Memory of Edward B. Irving, Jr.*, ed. Amodio and O'Keefe, 51. In the Old English, this phrase reads, "þæt soðe leoht, hælend crist, ðe onlihte ealne middaneard"; see Ælfric's "Alius Sermo De Die Paschae," ll. 220-21 in Godden, *Ælfric's Catholic Homilies: The Second Series Text*, EETS (London: Oxford University Press, 1979) 168, hereafter referred to as *The Second Series Text*.

[10]Godden, *Introduction, Commentary, and Glossary*, xxi. The author relies here and elsewhere on Clemoes's understanding that Ælfric had a comprehensive educational plan in mind as he wrote each piece in his large corpus. This scholar's analogy of Ælfric's works and a Gothic cathedral is also still helpful, especially when one considers the notion of the cathedral as frozen music and Ælfric's lifelong dedication to singing the *Opus Dei* and then turning its core into very Benedictine sermons. See Clemoes's seminal article, "The Chronology of Ælfric's Works," in *Old English Prose: Basic Readings*, ed. Szarmach, 57-

vernacular Ælfric explains Christianity's major doctrines, provides his audience commentary on them, and highlights Christ's crucial sacrifice as the sole way to salvation. The largest extant Old English prose text, these two volumes well represent the spirit of late Anglo-Saxon times.

Referred to as the First and Second Series, the *Catholic Homilies* are liturgical sermons combining the Temporale and Sanctorale. In each, Ælfric provided a sermon for approximately every second Sunday in a two-year cycle so a congregation could listen to a sermon twice monthly.[11] The First Series is chiefly scriptural and exegetical, and the Second is more hagiographical.[12] Dedicated to Sigeric, Archbishop of Canterbury (AD 990–994), and composed at the request of ealdorman Æthelweard and his son Æthelmaer, these vernacular sermons were written to be preached by learned and/or Latin-less priests during the section of the Mass called Prone, which followed the Gospel and in Carolingian times had developed as a fitting interlude for catechetical instruction. They may also have been intended as private devotional material for both the learned and those with no Latin.[13] Another yet unproven suggestion is that Ælfric may have first composed these two series for his own use in preaching at Cernel.[14]

---

58. It is also available in *The Anglo-Saxons*, ed. Clemoes, 212-47. For more background information on monastic singing, see Mary Berry, "What the Saxon Monks Sang: Music in Winchester in the Late Tenth Century," in *Bishop Æthelwold: His Career and Influence*, ed. Yorke, 149-60. Clemoes's 1959 article outlines Ælfric's canon, which Pope refines in his 1967–1968 edition. See "The Ælfric Canon," in *Homilies* I.136-45. Hereafter Clemoes's "Chronology" references the 1959 edition. The 2001 Sir Israel Gollancz Prize was given to the three-volume *Ælfric's Catholic Homilies* edited by the late Peter Clemoes and Malcolm Godden and published by the Early English Text Society (EETS). Many regard this triune edition—which began with Clemoes's Cambridge dissertation in 1955—as the major Old English publication in the last half of the twentieth century. See Godden, *The Second Series Text* (1979); Clemoes, *Ælfric's Catholic Homilies: The First Series Text*, EETS (Oxford: Oxford University Press, 1997), hereafter referred to as *The First Series Text*; and Godden, *Introduction, Commentary and Glossary* (2001).

[11]Green, "Ælfric the Catechist," 62.

[12]Stanley B. Greenfield and Daniel G. Calder, *A New Critical History of Old English Literature* (New York: New York University Press, 1986) 78. Compare Clemoes, Chronology," 229.

[13]See Gatch, *Preaching*, 37-38, 196. Gatch also discusses the use of the *Catholic Homilies* as private devotional material; see *Preaching*, 48-49.

[14]For the theory that Ælfric first wrote these homilies for his own use, see Norman Eliason and Peter Clemoes, eds., *Ælfric's First Series of Catholic Homilies. British Museum Royal 7 C. XII fols. 4-218*, EETS, Early English Manuscripts in Facsimile 13 (Copenhagen: Rosenkilde and Bagger, 1966) 28-29.

Malcolm Godden concludes, "What the *Catholic Homilies* were for is surprisingly difficult to say."[15]

Though Ælfric's audience is difficult to describe exactly, it is reasonable to imagine his primary target audience as the uneducated laity and their poorly educated preachers who could deliver the *Catholic Homilies* in lieu of understanding Latin themselves. Much in the *Catholic Homilies*, however, speaks to the specialized concerns of monks, the educated clergy, and the more learned laity (for example, the Gospel exegesis in most of Ælfric's sermons echoes practices of monastic devotion).[16] The apparent mixed nature of Ælfric's audience may reflect his own situation as monk, abbot, and scholar trying to communicate a long tradition of Christian learning to uneducated laity and priests as well as learned communities of monks, clergymen, and thanes, but, as Godden argues, it does seem Ælfric weighted his sermons towards the more learned in his audience or readership.[17]

Better perhaps than an elusive precise knowledge of Ælfric's audience is an understanding of the way this Anglo-Saxon monk wrote with his listeners always uppermost in his mind. Wilcox points out:

> The limits of the homiletic genre were imposed by the needs of the audience. . . . The mixed and all-encompassing audience gives Old English homilies a democratic stamp. Homilists created works intended for a broader audience than any other literature in Anglo-Saxon England, the learned and the unlearned. . . . Ælfric's homilies exemplify the work of a leading intellectual of his day carefully creating a reliable and clear body of significant doctrine so that it will be available for a mass audience.[18]

---

[15] Godden, *Introduction, Commentary, and Glossary*, xxi-xxii, xxv. Godden's conclusion is refreshing because it admits to the complexity of the question. In this same spirit, his introduction provides both a broad overview and an in-depth analysis of Ælfric's Catholic Homilies, their audience, historical milieu, date, and origin, alliterative style, and sources; see Godden, *Introduction, Commentary, and Glossary*, xxi-lxii.

[16] Ibid., xxvi-xxvii. Godden lists other reasons for this complexity of audience: The secular clergy also lived a community existence and were encouraged to maintain the same schedule of daily office, and Ælfric's homilies may reflect his own experience of preaching to combined audiences of monks and laity at Old Minster in Winchester, at Cerne, and elsewhere.

[17] Ibid., xxiii-xxiv. Godden convincingly argues Ælfric's having anticipated more learned people would read or hear his homilies. For a good example of Ælfric's writing to this point, see homily 22 ("In Letania Maiore Feria IIII") in Godden, *The Second Series Text*, 206ff.

[18] Wilcox, *Ælfric's Prefaces*, 21. Wilcox describes the Cerne Abbas scriptorium as "a

Grammar, Glossary, Colloquy, and De Temporibus Anni

Ælfric intended his *Grammar*, *Glossary*, and *Colloquy* to be a key part of his educational plan. He wrote these to help oblates learn how to speak, write, and dispute in Latin. Composed in Old English, Ælfric's Latin grammar (under the Latin title *Excerptiones de arte grammatica anglice*) draws on standard works of two Latin grammarians—Donatus's *Ars Grammatica (Maior)* and *Ars Minor* and Priscian's *Institutiones Grammaticae*. Ælfric's Latin grammar is the first written in English and also the first in any European vernacular.[19] He wrote it immediately after completing the First and Second Series of the *Catholic Homilies* and declares in it that grammar is "the key to unlocking . . . [their] . . . meaning."[20] Fifteen surviving manuscripts attest to the *Grammar*'s popularity as an Old English textbook for young boys learning Latin.[21]

Appended to seven of these copies is Ælfric's *Glossary*, a Latin-English dictionary consisting of several hundred Latin nouns and adjectives with their English equivalents. Arranged topically rather than alphabetically, the *Glossary* begins with God and the creation; then gives definitions of parts of the body, names of birds, fishes, and other animals; and concludes with characteristics of men. Ælfric's practical (or one could say Benedictine) pedagogical mind is obvious in his choosing this quotidian vocabulary.[22]

The third of Ælfric's Latin language aids is perhaps the most famous Old English prose text, though it is nothing more than a monastic schoolboy's required list of Latin vocabulary words. Composed in Latin,

---

small cottage industry" for producing and copying manuscripts of Ælfric's works and then distributing them throughout Canterbury and beyond, and he argues cogently that in this way Ælfric's sermons were adopted "as something of a national pastoral programme for the eleventh century." See his "Transmission of Literature and Learning: Anglo-Saxon Scribal Culture," in *A Companion to Anglo-Saxon Literature*, ed. Pulsiano and Treharne, 50-70.

[19]Greenfield and Calder, *A New Critical History*, 86; Caroline L. White, *Ælfric: A New Study of His Life and Writings*, Yale Studies in English II, ed. Albert S. Cook (Boston: Lamson, Wolffe and Co, 1898) 119. For more on the *Grammar*'s Latin manuscript title, see Wilcox, *Ælfric's Prefaces*, 36.

[20]Julius Zupitza, *Ælfrics Grammatik und Glossar* (Berlin: Weidmannsche Buchhandlung, 1880) 2.16-17; also quoted in Clemoes, "Ælfric," 190.

[21]G. I. Needham, ed., *Ælfric: Lives of Three English Saints*, Exeter Medieval English Texts, M. J. Swanton, gen. ed. (Exeter: University of Exeter, 1984) 13.

[22]This paragraph depends on Greenfield and Calder, *A New Critical History*, 75, 86-87.

the *Colloquy*'s dramatic tone, realism, social inclusiveness, splendid structure, energetic debates, clarity, and lively style distinguish it.[23] Ælfric created this vibrant snapshot of Anglo-Saxon society by transforming a mundane word list into an animated dialogue between teacher and cloistral pupils, with the pupils playfully assuming the roles of representatives of diverse occupations in Anglo-Saxon society.[24]

The continuous Old English gloss found in one of the four complete *Colloquy* manuscripts is not by Ælfric, but is the work, perhaps, of a cleric a generation or two after him.[25] Modern students learning Old English find the Ælfrician paronomasia of this gloss enlightening. The exchange between the 'farmer' (a cloistral student) and the teacher is one good example of this paronomasia, for it plays on three different meanings of the Old English word *hig*, which can denote 'hay,' the pronoun 'them,' or the expletive 'Hey!'

The 'farmer' explains his chores to his teacher: "Ic sceal fyllan binnan / oxan mid *hig*, ⁊ wæterian *hig*, ⁊ scearn heora beran ut" ("I have to fill the bin of the oxen with *hay*, and water *them*, and carry their dung away").[26] His instructor exclaims, "*Hig*! *Hig*! Micel gedeorf ys hyt" ("*Hey*! *Hey*! That's a huge task").[27] The 'farmer' creates the first pun in his use of *hig* to denote both 'hay' and the pronoun, 'them.' The teacher makes the second pun when he answers with the Old English expletive 'Hey!' (or 'Ha!'). Ælfric concludes the *Colloquy* on a serious note by reminding his monastic pupils the highest of all vocations is monkhood because it is a life spent serving God.

Ælfric's translation of Bede's *De Temporibus Anni* represents another first: the first work of astronomy in English. In it, Ælfric presents that essential medieval subject, cosmography, discussing the divisions of time and the solar year, as well as atmospheric phenomena, principles of astronomy, and information used to calculate the dates for church festivals, especially the rotating, much-debated date for Easter.[28]

---

[23]Ibid., 86.
[24]James Hurt, *Ælfric* (New York: Twayne Publishers, Inc., 1972) 35.
[25]Greenfield and Calder, *A New Critical History*, 87.
[26]G. N. Garmonsway, ed., *Colloquy*, 2nd ed., 1939 (Exeter: Exeter University Press, 1999) 21.33-34. The tironian notæ (⁊) in the quotation represent *and*.
[27]Ibid., 21.34.
[28]Needham, *Three English Saints*, 14.

Lives of Saints, Translations of the Bible, Pastoral Letters, and Vita S. Æthelwoldi

Ælfric's educational plan would not have been complete without his forty *Lives of Saints* (998), Old Testament narratives, Latin *Vita S. Æthelwoldi* (*Life of Æthelwold*), and 'occasional' writings (letters to thanes and others explaining fundamental Christian principles) because these provide his audience with models for and practical instructions on good Christian living.[29] Ælfric's *Lives of Saints* were written at the request of ealdorman Æthelweard and his son Æthelmaer, and—in contrast with the saints' lives presented in series one and two of Ælfric's *Catholic Homilies*—the ones in this later collection deal with saints whose feast days are honored only by the monks.[30] Ælfric probably considered his three collections (the two *Catholic Homilies* volumes and *Lives of Saints*) as a three-part series through which he first made available in the vernacular an account of and commentary on the major beliefs of Christianity, including the Scriptures, the origins and spread of the faith, and the stories of the martyrs.[31]

Lives of Saints were written for a more select audience than the *Catholic Homilies*. Ælfric felt it inappropriate to translate many of these saints' lives into English "because the pearls of Christ might be held in disrespect."[32] He intended *Lives* to be read—not aloud in church—but privately by a few select ecclesiastics and noblemen such as Æthelweard. Nonetheless, six of these forty works are sermons, and three works at the end of the volume appear to be separate from the rest: the *Interrogationes*, *De Falsis Diis*, and *De XII Abusivis*.[33]

Ælfric is also considered the first important translator of the Bible into English, though he was always a reluctant one. At Æthelweard's familiar insistence, however, he did translate much, though not all, of the Bible into the vernacular. He was always fearful his audience might misinterpret the Old Testament's polygamy and marriage of priests or that they would be unable to comprehend the spiritual meaning underlying the Bible's 'literal narrative.' He worried, "[I]f some unwise person reads this book, or hears

---

[29]Clemoes, "Chronology," 58, and Greenfield and Calder, *A New Critical History*, 76.
[30]Hurt, *Ælfric*, 35.
[31]Greenfield and Calder, *A New Critical History*, 76.
[32]Eric John, "The World of Abbot Ælfric," in *Ideal and Reality in Frankish and Anglo-Saxon Society*, ed. Wormald with Bullough and Collins, 302.
[33]Hurt, *Ælfric*, 35.

it read, he'll think he's allowed to live today under the new law as the ancient fathers lived before the old law was established or as people lived under Moses's law."[34]

Although Ælfric expresses opposition to translating God's sacred word from Latin into the vernacular, he did have precedents to follow: Bede has been credited with a translation of the Gospel of John, and a mid-tenth-century West Saxon version of the Gospels existed.[35] Ælfric's biblical translations fall into three categories: paraphrases and epitomes of several books, such as Job, Kings, the Maccabees, Esther, Judith, Judges, and Joshua; translations of individual passages (mainly Gospel pericopes in his sermons); and an extended literal translation of certain chapters of Genesis (1-3, 6-9, 11-24) and Numbers (13-26).[36]

Ælfric also wrote letters to bishops and archbishops and thanes, and these provide additional Christian instruction in an obviously pastoral fashion. His *Letter for Wulfsige* outlines the duties of the clergy (and was composed for the Bishop of Sherborne), and his *Letters for Wulfstan* (written for and at the request of the archbishop of York and bishop of Worcester) contain much of the same subject matter, plus directions for the celebration of Passion Week, expositions of the Ten Commandments and the eight deadly sins, and exhortations to the clergy to live a life of celibacy. The letters to Wulfstan were first composed in Latin, but a year later were translated into the vernacular at the archbishop's insistence. Ælfric's *Letter To Wulfgeat*, written to a leading landowner near Eynsham, briefly describes the basics of Christianity, and concludes by encouraging Wulfgeat to "agree with your adversary." At the request of another prominent but untutored thane, Sigeweard of Easthealon, Ælfric wrote one of his most complete synopses of Christian doctrine, often titled *On the Old and New Testaments*.[37]

---

[34]Greenfield and Calder, *A New Critical History*, 84-85. In the Old English: "gif sum dysig man þæs boc ræt oððe rædon gehyrð, þæt he wille wenan þæt he mote lybban nu on þære niwan æ, swa swa þa ealdan fæderas leofodon þa on þæra tide, ær þan þe seo ealde æ gesett wære, oððe swa swa men leofodon under Moyses æ."

[35]Ibid., 84. See Roy M. Liuzza, ed., *The Old English Version of the Gospels*, EETS OS 304, 314 (Oxford: Oxford University Press, 1994, 2000) and Liuzza with A. N. Doane, eds., *Anglo-Saxon Manuscripts in Microfiche Facsimile*, vol. 6: *Gospels* (Binghamton NY: Medieval and Renaissance Texts and Studies, 1995).

[36]Greenfield and Calder, *A New Critical History*, 84.

[37]This paragraph on Ælfric's letters depends on the following sources: Greenfield and Calder, *A New Critical History*, 87-88; Hurt, *Ælfric*, 36, 38-41; Stenton, *Anglo-Saxon*

Ælfric's Latin *Letter to the Monks of Eynsham* presents detailed liturgical instructions and a rare glimpse into the world of ordinary Benedictine monks. In it, Ælfric shows a Benedictine impulse to simplify: he streamlines some of the more elaborate (and more famous) rites of the *Regularis Concordia Anglicae nationis monachorum sanctimonialiumque*, an early 970s' landmark in religious legislation detailing the liturgical routine to be followed by all English monks: for example, Ælfric lessens the *Concordia*'s emphasis on the royal patronage of monasticism.[38] His Latin *Vita S. Æthelwoldi* (*Life of St. Æthelwold*) is a fitting late composition honoring Ælfric's early spiritual mentor.

By the end of his life, Ælfric's corpus was as immense as it was impressive. Its pedagogical clarity, polished language, clean stylistic lines, and unique rhythmical prose have attracted scholars and intelligent readers throughout the centuries. Significantly, Ælfric never stopped revising, reissuing, and extending his earlier work. He viewed this creation of pedagogical materials as an ongoing process, like the forgiveness and salvation they teach.

The sermons translated in this book represent Ælfric's best work. Five (VII-X, XII) were written between the completion of *Lives* (998) and the beginning of Ælfric's abbacy (1005).[39] Six others (I, XIII-XVII) were likely written after 1005, and XIV may be as late as 1009 or 1010.[40] A few are earlier. Pope suggests sermon IV is "roughly contemporary" with *Lives* (998), and sermons II-III and V-VI may have been issued before *Lives*.[41] The later dates accorded most of these translated sermons show Ælfric never stopped creating new pieces.

England, 668; and Wilcox, *Ælfric's Prefaces*, 54-55.

[38] For more information on this landmark religious legislation, see Dom Thomas, ed. and trans., *Regularis Concordia Anglicae Nationis Monachorum Sanctimonialiumque: The Monastic Agreement of the Monks and Nuns of the English Nation* (London: Thomas Nelson and Sons, Ltd., 1953) ix. Christopher A. Jones' *Ælfric's Letter to the Monks of Eynsham* (Cambridge: Cambridge University Press, 1999) contains a new edition of the Latin text with a critical apparatus and is the only complete English translation. Jones' introductory chapters establish the importance of this letter for our understanding of late Anglo-Saxon monasticism and liturgy. For details about Ælfric's changes in his consuetudinary, see Milton McC. Gatch, "The Office in Late Anglo-Saxon Monasticism," in *Learning and Literature in Anglo-Saxon England*, eds. Lapidge and Gneuss, 349.

[39] Pope, *Homilies* I.147-49.
[40] Ibid., 148.
[41] Ibid., 148-49, 226-27.

The Influence of the Rule of St. Benedict on Ælfric

Ælfric's importance as writer, teacher, scholar, and theologian is well established, but this very assertion introduces a Western love of ranking which risks misleading the reader and sidetracking a modern audience away from Ælfric's real purpose. The rare scholarly accord praising Ælfric should be set aside a moment to allow for a reexamination of the raison d'etre of this Benedictine monk. Since Ælfric is known for his use of the commonplace to teach the spiritual extraordinary (as when he famously compares Christ's divinity and humanity with the separate blendedness of egg white and egg yolk in "Sermo de Natale Domini),"[42] it seems appropriate to use an ordinary object lesson to characterize Ælfric and his work.

This Anglo-Saxon Benedictine monk's simple, graceful, inclusive theology finds contemporary expression in an experience I had at one of Western Michigan University's International Medieval Congresses in Kalamazoo. Through Sister Linda Kulzer of the Benedictine community of St. John's Abbey (Collegeville, Minnesota), I met the Reverend John Crean, Sister Judith Sutera, Sister Teresa Wolking, Sister Mary Forman, Father Hugh Feiss, Sister Deborah Harmeling, and others, and through them discovered a direct link to the spirit pervading Ælfric's work. Their ordinary, hospitable paths teach the Benedictine way. They listen. They share their lives, their rented cars, their deep knowledge of *The Rule of St. Benedict*, their snacks, and even their money, for the American Benedictine Academy session is one of the few at Kalamazoo giving stipends to presenters.

And my Benedictine colleagues are—contrary to stereotype—hardly dull. I remember a lively debate at supper about the medieval women mystics, and the general nun-consensus was Julian of Norwich was never a recluse in the way some outside the cloister assume but that she did have a marvelous grasp of what nuns like to call "the ordinary," while Margery Kempe was not applauded because she was considered far too weepy and enamored of "extraordinary" spiritual experiences. They also introduced

---

[42]Benjamin Thorpe, ed. and trans., *The Homilies of the Anglo-Saxon Church. The First Part, Containing the Sermones Catholici, or Homilies of Ælfric. In the Original Anglo-Saxon, with an English Version*, 2 vols., Ælfrices Bocgild (London: Richard and John E. Taylor, 1844, 1846) I.41, hereafter referred to as *Homilies*. As with Pope, the roman numeral indicates volume, and the Arabic numeral the page number. See unnumbered line 10 up from the bottom.

me to the engaging Dame Frevisse in the vivid medieval mysteries of Edgar-award-nominated author Margaret Frazer.

One May, I entered Western Michigan University's teeming Valley III cafeteria holding a tray of barbequed chicken leg, institution-white rice, and asparagus, and scanned the dining room for a friendly face. Remembering my monastic friends' habit of sitting on the right side of this boisterous room, I shifted my gaze and spotted them at once. Then I noticed with disappointment their circular table was crowded with seven sisters and no empty chairs.

No room for me, I thought, and began looking elsewhere, but I had been spotted. When elderly Sister Teresa Wolking raised an arm in welcome, I shuffled towards their table, still uncertain. Sister Deborah Harmeling rose to meet me with a smile, then disappeared behind my back, and as she left—in one motion—the others took their plates off cement-dull cafeteria trays and stowed these trays under their seats. All this fuss made me ask, "You sure there's room?" and Sister Deborah answered my question by returning with a chair and placing it firmly under me: "There's always room at a round table."

There's always room at a round table echoed in my head as I unloaded my own plates and stowed the tray under the gift of my chair, and joined the community. This is Ælfric's world. The Benedictine idea of Christian community and the blessing of the ordinary (in this case, a chair) is the very foundation of the sermons written by our most prolific, 'best' Old English sermonizer. Because Ælfric's large corpus rests in this gentle spirit of *The Rule of St. Benedict*, to understand Ælfric's writings, then, it is first necessary to read and appreciate the prologue and seventy-three brief chapters of Benedict's sixth-century Latin *Rule*, which teaches the monastic virtues of obedience, silence, hospitality, chastity, diligence, nonviolent behavior, and humility, as well as outlines times for the *Opus Dei*, meals, meditative reading (*lectio*), and manual labor.

The *Rule*'s most lasting attraction is its signature ordinary quality. This spiritual guide was not designed for mystics or superhumans but for the average person wanting to commune with God. Though originally written for those living in medieval monasteries, today its practical spiritual wisdom attracts readers and followers from every walk of life.[43]

---

[43] See Joan Chittister, *Wisdom Distilled from the Daily: Living the Rule of St. Benedict Today* (San Francisco: HarperSanFrancisco, 1991) and *The Rule of Benedict: Insight for the Ages* (New York: Crossroad Pub. Co., 1992); also Esther de Waal and Kathleen Norris,

The *Rule* begins with a call to obedience and listening, and modern Benedictine monks and nuns are indeed, in my experience, regular people who are extraordinary listeners. Sister Linda Kulzer is a spiritual director (or mentor) at St. John's Abbey, and in our interactions she certainly practices "holy listening," as the famous prologue teaches:

> Listen, Child of God, to your teacher's wisdom. Pay attention to what your heart hears. Make sure you freely accept and live out the loving Father's directions. The work of obedience is the way to return to Christ when the carelessness of disobedience has made you stray. My words are meant for you specifically, whoever and wherever you are, wanting to turn from your own self-will and join Christ, the Lord of all. Follow him by wearing the powerful, sacred shield of submission. Pray first before you do any worthwhile work. Then persist and never weaken in prayer. God loves us as his own sons and daughters and forgives us, so we must not grieve him by rejecting that love and doing evil. We must always make the best use of the good things God gives us.[44]

The main themes of Ælfric's large corpus are reflected in these opening instructions of the *Rule*, and its caring fatherly tone is also a trait of Ælfric's prose. The most important shared motif is *Listen*. Pay attention to God's words. (For Ælfric, as we have seen, that also meant *Know your*

Seeking God: The Way of St. Benedict, 2nd ed. (Collegeville MN: Liturgical Press, 2001).

[44] Verses 1-6a. Although this modern translation does not mimic the masculine language of the Latin one read by Ælfric, it has timeless appeal and true Benedictine inclusiveness. I recommend the following versions of the *Rule*: Timothy Fry, O.S.B., ed., *RB1980: The Rule of St. Benedict in English: In Latin and English with Notes* (Collegeville MN: Liturgical Press, 1981), a standard masculine version; Leonard Doyle, trans., *The Rule of St. Benedict* (Collegeville MN: Liturgical Press, 2001); Terrence G. Kardong, *Benedict's Rule: A Translation and Commentary* (Collegeville MN: Liturgical Press, 1996), with its keen commentary; Mayeul de Dreuille, O.S.B., *The Rule of Saint Benedict: A Commentary in Light of World Ascetic Traditions* (New York: Paulist Press, 2002), and its global context; Patrick Barry, O.S.B., *Saint Benedict's Rule: A New Translation for Today* (Herefordshire: Ampleforth Abbey Press, 1997), for its inclusive language; and H. Logeman, ed., *Saint Benedict of Nursia. The Rule of S. Benet: Latin and Anglo-Saxon Interlinear Version*, London, 1888 (n.p.: Elibron Classics Series, 2003) for an Anglo-Saxon version. See the *Rule* online at the site of the Order of St. Benedict at St. John's Abbey, Collegeville, Minnesota, with multilingual translations and bibliographic information at <http://www.osb.org/rb/index.html#English>. For more information on Ælfric's adherence to the *Rule*, see Gatch, *Preaching*, 104. Joseph P. McGowan discusses Benedictine reformer Dunstan's introduction of *The Rule of St. Benedict* while abbot at Glastonbury: see "An Introduction to the Corpus of Anglo-Latin Literature," in *A Companion to Anglo-Saxon Literature*, ed. Pulsiano and Treharne, 38.

audience.) Other Benedictine principles found both here and in Ælfric's corpus are equally active: Be obedient. Surrender your will. Turn to Christ. Pray. Repent. Battle the evil within your own soul. And use God's good gifts to please him with your actions.

Ælfric recognized that the power of Benedict's *Rule* resides in its simplicity and brevity. He knew the wisdom of its last sentence (the "Epilogue"): "Whoever you are rushing to your heavenly home, follow with Christ's help *this little* [literally, "minimum"] *rule* we've written for beginners. Only then, with God watching over you, will you eventually reach the soaring heights of doctrine and goodness."[45]

Shaped as Ælfric's sermons are by the wisdom of Benedict's "little rule," it is interesting that this Anglo-Saxon monk describes the first command Eden-rich Adam and Eve broke as "þæt lytle bebod" ("that little rule / commandment"), an Old English phrase echoing "this little rule" of Benedict's epilogue. In sermon XXI, "De Falsis Diis" Ælfric writes:

> Ne hungor ne þurst, ne hefigtyme cyle, / ne nan swidhlic hæte, ne seocnyss ne mihton / Adam geswencan on þam earde, / þa hwile þe he *þæt lytle bebod* mid geleafan geheold.

> (Neither hunger nor thirst nor bitter cold / nor overwhelming heat nor sickness could / torment Adam on this earth, / so long as he faithfully kept *that little commandment*.)[46]

Perhaps in this striking Old English echo of the *Rule*'s epilogue Ælfric is laying bare his entire theological argument. As Benedict's prologue points out, the child of God finds following submission's path simple; the only 'hard' thing is stubborn self-will: "The work of obedience is the way to return to Christ when the carelessness of disobedience has made you stray." Ælfric viewed obedience as a comfort, not a daunting divine request, and his framing the Fall of Man as Adam and Eve's breaking "þæt lytle bebod" ("that little commandment") shows the core of his mercy-focused Benedictine theology.

---

[45] Chap. 73, v. 8; italics added. Compare chap. 73, v. 8 in Doyle, *The Rule of St. Benedict*, 154, and Fry, *RB1980*, 651. I thank Brother Anthony of Seoul's Sogang University for an illuminating conversation about Benedict's "little" *Rule*. Its Latin epilogue reads: "Quisquis ergo ad patriam caelestem festinas, hanc minimam inchoationis regulam descriptam, adiuvante Christo, perfice, et tunc demum ad maiora quae supra commemoravimus doctrinae virtutumque culmina, Deo protegente, pervenies. Amen."

[46] Pope, *Homilies* II.678-79 (XXI.41-4); italics added.

Ælfric understood the Ur-*bebod* God gave Adam and Eve as being—to put it in the vernacular—"not a big deal." Instead, God's first "little commandment" was synonymous with (and also a type of) the reassuring words spoken by God's Son: "Come to me, all you who are weary and burdened, and I will give you rest. . . . For my yoke is easy and my burden is light" (Matthew 11.28-30) like Benedict's "little rule." In Ælfric's Benedictine mind, God's first "little commandment" and the later "little rule" of Benedict were separated only by time, not by spirit, because Ælfric understood and taught God the Father did (through Christ) and will do (through the Holy Spirit) most of the work for his children who desire spiritual growth; all that is left is humility through repentance, and kindness by doing good.

A study of the influence on Ælfric of *The Rule of St. Benedict* is a large lacuna in Old English scholarship and deserves close attention. Another interesting comparison could be made between Benedict's positive simplification of *The Rule of the Master*—that main source for his *Rule*—with Ælfric's quite similar positive adaptation and simplification of his patristic sources in his own sermons (and, as mentioned earlier, his own simplification of the *Concordia* in his Latin *Letter to the Monks of Eynsham*). A thorough analysis of Ælfric's teaching in light of the *Rule* would require more room than this introduction allows, but such an analysis would center Ælfrician scholarship in ways this Benedictine monk would certainly have approved.[47]

Ælfric on Good and Evil

The core of Ælfric's theology is praising God's generous goodness. He often describes God's democratic giving:

> Because of his goodness, God has given us the light of the sun as a lamp during the day, and God also gives us the moon and the stars to light our way at night, and he even gives us various good things to eat. He gives us our food: birds and fishes living in the waters and nourishing wild animals living in the woods. Because of God's great generosity, he has given us all things in common, to the rich and to the poor. Anyone who can catch the animals can eat them.[48]

---

[47]Christopher A. Jones and Lynne Grundy come closest to discussing the *Rule*'s influence on Ælfric when they both emphasize he was—in his own eyes—first a teacher, not a writer. See Jones, *Ælfric's Letter to the Monks*, 1ff., and Grundy, *Books and Grace: Ælfric's Theology*, King's College London Medieval Studies VI (London: King's College, 1991) 2ff.

[48]Pope, *Homilies* I.206 (I.206-14). In the Old English: "₇ God us . . . geuðe for his

Ælfric also carefully articulates the patristic view that God created nothing bad or evil:

> And no sin and no bad behavior and nothing evil was ever created by God. . . . Evil has no home. It has no place to live that allows it to exist anywhere except in created things that were created for good. God created the angels for good, and evil was not yet living anywhere; but then they found it and got lost through it.[49]

This, Ælfric explains, is how evil entered the good world. Angels created for good chose to disobey God, becoming evil.

Warring against the good God, then, is that most sublime and intelligent but disobedient of angels, Satan; and these are the two antipodal forces in Ælfric's universe. God has given his creation, man, free will to choose between these two, as Ælfric points out, "[E]very person has a free will and can choose what to love during his or her lifetime."[50] In other words, as Ælfric says in his "Sermon to the People, Delivered on the Octave of Pentecost" (XI), God created the first man "[so] he could have always existed without sinning, and without death, if only he had obeyed his Lord"; but, he adds, "Then the old devil came, filled with hatred, and deceived Adam the first man and he sinned against God and broke his commandment. And then Adam became mortal, and all of his descendants, too."[51]

---

godnesse / þære sunnan leoht to leohtfæte on dæge / ₇ monan ₇ steorran us mannum on niht / ₇ menigfealde bricas to urum bigleofan: / fixas ₇ fugelas þe on flodum wuniað, / ₇ þa wildan deor þe on wudum eardiað, / þa þe clæne syndon, mid his micclan cyste / he forgeaf us gemænlice eallum, / ricum ₇ heanum, þe heora hentan magon."

[49]Ibid., I.205 (I.183-84, 190-94). In the Old English: "Næs næfre nan synn þurh God gesceapen, / ne nan unrihtwisnyss ne yfel þurh hine. . . . / Næfð yfel nane wununge þæt hit wesan mæge / ahwær buton on gesceaftum þe gode wæron gesceapene. / Gode wæron þa englas from Gode gesceapene / ₇ þæt yfel næs þa gyt nahwær wunigende, / ac hi hit afundon, ₇ forferdon þurh þæt."

[50]Ibid., I.253 (III.113-14): "Ælc man hæfð agenne cyre / hwæt he lufige on his lifes timan."

[51]Ibid., I.419-20 (XI.95-97, 103-106). In the Old English: "þæt he beon mihte butan synnum æfre, / and eac butan deaðe, gif he his Drihtne gehyrde. . . . Ða com se ealda deofol mid andan afylled, / and beswac ðone mann, þæt he syngode wið God, / and his bebod tobræc þe he him bebead to healdenne, / and he wearð ða deadlic, and eall his offspring syððan." Cf. Pope, *Homilies* I.274 (IV.190).

Ælfric on Grace, Forgiveness, and a Personal Trinity

As seen in this passage quoted from "Sermon to the People," Ælfric clearly accepts the notion of original sin. He does not, however, emphasize this doctrine; instead, as some of the medieval women mystics who built on the fine prose tradition Ælfric continued (Julian of Norwich and Hildegard of Bingen come to mind), he constantly shifts the weight of his argument to the positive doctrines of grace and forgiveness.

The optimistic nature of Ælfric's sermons is particularly evidenced in his many paeans to the Trinity. This Benedictine monk presents the triune God as a Friend one can know, rather than an intellectual concept one might merely ponder. Ælfric's sermons often praise the unity of God the Father, God the Son, and God the Holy Spirit for making, loving, and saving the world with the most comforting forgiveness.[52]

In one of these lyrical passages from sermon VI, Ælfric sings of the Trinity:

> The almighty Father, who created all things, has one Son born ineffably from him alone, the true Savior. And the Holy Spirit is not called Son because he is one Father always without beginning, and his only begotten Son is of himself always, and the Holy Spirit is Will and Love of them both, ever with them and equally of them both. Now the Father is not Father of them both because one of them is his Son, and the other is not his Son. Again, the same Son is not Son of them both, that is, of the Father and of the Spirit, in the godhead. But the Holy Spirit alone is common to both of them, to the almighty Father and to his only begotten Son, and through that Spirit all sins are forgiven. . . . And he gives forgiveness to penitent persons and illuminates their minds with his gentle forgiveness and afterwards comforts them, because he is the Spirit of Comfort.[53]

---

[52]For examples, see Pope, *Homilies* I.201, I. 204 (I.84-97, 157-66); I.322-33 (VI.228-68); I.418 (XI.78-89); I.462-63, 471-72 (XIa.1-19, 197-234).

[53]Ibid., I.322-24 (VI.228-42, 251-53). In the Old English: "Se ælmihtiga Fæder, þe ealle ðing gesceop, / hæfð ænne Sunu of him anum acenned / unasecgendlice, þone soðfæstan Hælend; / and se Halga Gast nis na gehaten Sunu, / for ðan þe se an Fæder is æfre unbegunnen, / and his ancenneda Sunu of him sylfum æfre, / and se Halga Gast is heora begra Willa and Lufu, / æfre hiom betwynan, of hiom bam gelice. / Nu nis se Fæder heora begra fæder, / for ðan þe heora oðer is suna, and se oðer nis na suna. / Eft se ylca Sunu nis na heora begra suna, / þæs Fæder and þæs Gastes, on ðære godcundnesse. / Ac se Halga Gast ana is heom bam gemænelice, / ðam ælmihtigan Fæder and his ancennedan Suna, / and ðurh ðone Gast beoð ealle synna forgyfene. / . . . and he deð forgyfenysse ðam dædbetendum

Ælfric teaches each person's responsibility is simply to respond to God's grace and "gentle forgiveness" made especially evident when God the Father sent his Son to earth, to redeem humanity. This central theme of Christianity is written in large letters across Ælfric's corpus. In his straightforward preaching of the literal 'good news' of the Gospel, Ælfric is one of the most remarkable Christian evangelists of all time.[54]

Ælfric on Good Deeds

A noteworthy aspect of Ælfric's theology is the importance of being generous to the poor, and the seventeen sermons translated in this book well represent this penitential teaching. Ælfric writes that showing the poor mercy is showing Christ mercy: "The test of love is doing good works. In other words, God wants us to act, so we can always honor him with our good works—not by naked words with no action—because love is shown through action."[55]

Ælfric's definition of *love* is "kind action": "And if love isn't willing to work, then it isn't love."[56] No person, however, does good on his or her own strength or merit, as Ælfric explains to his congregation, "[W]e don't possess even one stick or one staff, or one eucharistic wafer for the good

---

mannum, / and heora mod onliht mid his liðan forgyfennysse, / and hi syððan gefrefrað, for ðan ðe he is Frofergast."

Cf. Pope, *Homilies* I.216 (I.470-72); I.242 (II.290-91); I.255-56 (III.176-87); I.273 (IV.163-72); I.365-66, 368 (VIII.186-204, 252-55); I.382-84 (IX.83-95, 110-23); I.405 (X.207-11); I.446-7 (XI.566-74); II.489 (XII.235-41); and II.559 (XVI.286-95).

[54]For a few examples of the numerous evangelistic passages in *God of Mercy*, see Pope, *Homilies* I.324 (VI.262-65), I.212-14 (I.386-90, 404-409); I.233-35 (II.73-74, 98-100); I.253, 256 (III.124-32, 177, 180-81); I.273-75, 279 (IV.175, 179, 202, 267-68); I.293 (V.102-113); I.344-45 (VII.86-89, 111-12); I.366 (VIII.200-202); I.381 (IX.60-63); I.404-405 (X.199-200, 207-10); I.415-17 (XI.6-53); I.463, 465-66 (XIa.4-5, 53-56, 75-78); II.487-89 (XII.200-202, 234-38); II.503 (XIII.136-40); II.517-18 (XIV.51-65); II.533 (XV.49); II.557 (XVI.243-47); II.569-70, 576, 580 (XVII.71-77, 215-19, 306-13).

[55]Ibid., I.397 (X.31-35). In the Old English: "Þære lufe fandung is þæs weorces fremming, þæt is þæt God wile þa weorc habban æt us, þæt we mid godum weorcum hine wurðian a, na mid nacodum wordum butan þære fremminge, for ðan þe seo lufu sceall beon geswutelod mid dædum." Compare Pope, *Homilies* I.439 (XI.426-34), where eternal reward or punishment is tied to an abundance or a lack of almsgiving.

[56]Ibid., I.398 (X.61). In the Old English: "[A]nd gif heo [lufu] wyrcan nele, nis heo þone lufu."

of our Mass if God himself hadn't provided it for us at an earlier time. Yet we can use God's own things and make him pleased with us."[57]

Contrasting Sermonizers: Ælfric and Wulfstan

Ælfric's work differs significantly from other Old English sermons because he consistently affirms God's mercy. God is kind, Ælfric teaches. Ælfric does not shirk from describing hell's reality and terrors, but neither does he dwell on these to create in his audience the fear of God's punishment, as his colleague Archbishop Wulfstan clearly does in *Sermo Lupi ad Anglos*.[58] Nor does Ælfric shock like an earlier Blickling homily when it declares a person's decomposing body "the food of worms" which "issue from each joint."[59] Ælfric does not try to frighten his audience into repentance and confession.

Wulfstan's famous *Sermo Lupi ad Anglos* is well known for its threats.[60] It begins on a menacing note, lists one English fault after another, harping throughout on hell's answering awfulness, then concludes with a final reminder of the fire disobedience deserves. The excerpts below communicate its scathing flavor:

> Dear People, surely you see the truth of what I'm saying. Our world is hurtling to its End, and the longer things continue like this, the worse they'll get. Our world is a mess because people sin day after day. We live in a terribly dangerous time, in the period before the coming of the Antichrist; and, yes, all of earth will end in an awful manner. Come to grips with that right now, for the Devil has long made this nation wander way off God's path. There's little loyalty among men, though they speak well. . . . And everyone is stingy, injustice is epidemic, and everyone loves breaking the law. Worst of all, God's laws are hated, his teaching is scorned, and that's why God's anger damns our days. Hear this—if you can—and believe it. Though you may not believe it, all

---

[57]Ibid., I.207 (I.251-5). In the Old English: "Ne furðon ænne sticcan ne ænne stæf we næfdon / ne ane oflætan to urum mæssan gode / gyf he us ne foresceawode him sylf þæt in ær; / ₇ we magon swaþeah mid his agenum þingum hine us gegladian." This Ælfrician passage especially echoes verse 6a of the *Rule*'s prologue, quoted earlier: "We must always make the best use of the good things God gives us."

[58]Allen J. Frantzen, *The Literature of Penance in Anglo-Saxon England* (New Brunswick: Rutgers University Press, 1983) 162.

[59]R. Morris, *The Blickling Homilies of the Tenth Century*, 1874–1880, EETS OS 58 (Woodbridge: Boydell & Brewer, 1997) 111, 101. See sermons X (l. 33) and VIII (ll. 2-8).

[60]Dorothy Bethurum, "Wulfstan," in Continuations and Beginnings: Studies in Old English Literature, ed. Eric G. Stanley (London: Thomas Nelson and Sons, Ltd., 1966) 215.

will be lost, unless God protects us. It's obvious we've been sinning more than confessing, which is why our nation is punished. For a long time, nothing has succeeded here or abroad. We've known only war, hunger, fire, and bloodshed in every district, without end. We suffer stealing, murders, plagues, hunger, hatred, robberies, and looting. And we are also helpless under heavy taxes and crop-spoiling storms. In this land we've had years of instability because of widespread disloyalty. . . . None of us lived as we should. . . . We must constantly think about the great Day of Judgment we'll experience before we know it. Today we must defend ourselves against hell's gathering, tormenting fires. We must earn the glories and delights God has prepared for those who work his will in this world. God help us! Amen.[61]

Allen J. Frantzen points out that *Sermo Lupi ad Anglos* is not so much about penance as about the nation's negative actions to avoid it: "The

---

[61]Dorothy Whitelock, "The Anglo-Saxon Achievement," in *History, Law, and Literature in 10th–11th Century England*, Collected Studies Series 128 (London: Variorum Reprints, 1981) 33. Also see Melissa J. Bernstein's *Electronic Sermo Lupi Ad Anglos* (New York: University of Rochester) at <http://www.cif.rochester.edu/%7Emjbernst/wulfstan/sermo_index.html> (cited 9 September 2004). For examples of Ælfric's preaching on the Antichrist, see Clemoes, *The First Series Text*, 175; Wilcox, *Ælfric's Prefaces*, 109; and Thorpe, *Homilies* I.4.14-21, I.4.30, and I.6.16 ("Preface"), where Ælfric uses very strong language: "se wælhreowa antecrist" ("the blood-thirsty Antichrist"). In the Old English, the excerpts from Wulfstan read: "Leofan men gecnawað þæt soð is: ðeos worolde is on ofste & hit nealæcð þam ende. & þy hit is on worolde aa swa leng swa wyrse, & swa hit sceal nyde for folces synnan fram dæge to dæge, ær antecristes tocyme, yfelian swyþe. & huru hit wyrð þænne egeslic & grimlic wide on worolde. Understandað eac georne þæt deofol þas þeode nu fela geara dwelode to swyþe & þæt lytle getreowþa wæran mid mannum, þeah hy wel spræcan. . . . Ælc man gelitla Ælc man gelitlað oððe forhealdeð, forðam unriht is to wide mannum gemæne & unlaga leofe. & hrædest is to cweþenne Godes laga laðe & lara forsawenne, & þæs we habbað ealle þurh Godes yrre bysmor gelome, gecnawe se þe cunne. & se byrst wyrð gemæne þeh man swa ne wene eallre þysse þeode butan God beorge. Forþam hit is on us eallum swutol & gesene þæt we ær þysan oftor bræcan þonne we bettan, & þy is þysse þeode fela onsæge. Ne dohte hit nu lange inne ne ute: ac wæs here & hungor, nu bryne & blodgyte on gewelhwylcan ende oft & gelome. & us stalu & cwalu, stric & steorfa, orfcwealm & uncoþu, hol & hete, & rypera reaflac derede swyþe þearle. & us ungylda swyðe gedrohtan, & us unwedera foroft weoldan unwæstma; forþam on þysan earde wæs, swa hit þincan mæg, nu fela geara unrihta fela & tealte getrywða æghwær mid mannum. . . . Ne ænig wið oþerne getrywlice þohte swa rihte swa he scolde . . . & utan gelome understandan þone miclam Dom þe we ealle to sculon & beorgan us georne wið þone weallendan bryne helle wites, & geearnian us þa mærþa & þa myrhða þe God hæfð gegearwod þam þe his willan on worolde gewyrcað. God ure helpe, Amen."

homily catalogues sins in mounting numbers, leaving only the faintest hope that the people will turn from their evil ways."[62]

Ælfric does chide, but more gently. At lines 98-107 and 127-39 in the sermon for the sixth Sunday after Pentecost (XIV), he presents what Pope says is perhaps his "severest" reproof to the English, though even this rare indictment has a sober tone and is tempered by a reminder of God's goodness and each person's ability to obey him:[63]

> But here in the English nation we feebly keep the laws God established to guide and instruct all those who love him. Instead, we create for ourselves new laws entirely different from those God himself taught. These laws are contrary to God's laws and to those of all the wise men who lived before us. With our self-will we rebel against them all. By trampling on God's laws with bad behavior and despising our Lord, as we are doing, we will make the way very difficult for ourselves. . . . So many people submit along with the chosen ones to Christ's faith in his church, that later some of them break out in an evil manner. And they spend their lives in errors—as the English people do who submit to the Danes—and they are branded by Satan for evil service. And they do the devil's deeds to the destruction of themselves, and they betray their own people to death. Think about this. Is there anything worse than such a betrayal committed against one's own Lord? No, there is nothing worse because it causes the betrayer to fall into eternal torments, estranged from God and all his saints.[64]

The main difference between these two master rhetoricians is obvious. Wulfstan accuses his hearers of sinfulness and promises a horror-filled hell

---

[62]Frantzen, *Literature of Penance*, 162.
[63]Pope, *Homilies* II.512.
[64]Ibid., II.519-20 (XIV.98-107) and II.521 (XIV.127-39). As noted earlier, Pope dates sermon XIV as written perhaps in 1009 or 1010, making it the latest of the seventeen sermons translated here; *Homilies* I.148-49. In the Old English, these Ælfrician passages read: "Ac we healdað wace, her on Engla þeode, / Godes gesetnyssa, þe he gesette to steore, / and þam eallum to lare þe hine lufiað. / We wyrcað us sylfe eall-niwe gesetnyssa / of ðam þe God sylf tæhte, ongean his gesetnyssum, / and ealra þæra witena þe wæron beforan us, / ongean hy ealle we gað mid ure anwilnysse; / ac se weg sceal beon swiðe earfoðe us, / þæt we hy fortredon mid teonfullum þeawum, / and God sylfne forseon, swa swa we to swiðe doð. . . . / An nu bið eac swa. / Swa fela manna gebugað mid ðam gecorenum / to Cristes geleafan on his Gelaðunge, / þæt hy sume yfele eft ut abrecað, / and hy on gedwyldum adreogað heora lif, / swa swa þa Engliscan men doð þe to ðam Deniscum gebugað, / and mearciað hy deofle to his mannrædene, / and his weorc wyrcað, hym sylfum to forwyrde, / and heora agene leode belæwað to deaðe. / Hwæt, bið æfre wyrse ænig þing on worlde / þonne swylce dæd is ongean his agene Drihten, / and hine sylfne besence on ðam ecum suslum, / ælfremed fram Gode, and fram eallum his halgum?"

he then forces them to contemplate by listing these terrors vividly (very like the eighteenth-century Calvinistic preacher, Jonathan Edwards, in "Sinners in the Hands of an Angry God," and with the same result—a terrified congregation). Wulfstan aims to stimulate obedience through fear.

Ælfric's God of Mercy

On the other hand, Ælfric's "severest reproof" in sermon XIV is brief, and it is nestled in his calm exegesis of Luke 5:1-11, which teaches about Jesus's miraculous intervention that resulted in the huge catch of fishes, a miracle foreshadowing the disciples' future spiritual success in attracting many to Christ's teachings. Ælfric's short reproof has a positive context, then. During it, Ælfric also chooses to make a subtle appeal to his listeners' better nature, for in this calm admonition he includes a reminder of God's mercy: "[W]e feebly keep the laws God established to guide and instruct all those who love him." Ælfric has clearly decided not to frighten his audience with a snapshot of hell; instead, he asks them (and himself) to contemplate spiritual errors and realize disobedience makes "the way very difficult." This simple *difficult* is the only adjective Ælfric uses here. He seems to trust his audience to supply the personal details and, with God's grace, to correct them.

Wulfstan favors finger-pointing commands: "[A]nd, yes, all of earth will end in an awful manner. Come to grips with that right now, for the Devil has long made this nation wander way off God's path." His sweeping negative use of "we," "our," and "us" has the desired alarming affect in rebukes like this: "We must constantly think about the great Day of Judgment we'll experience before we know it." Ælfric, on the other hand, prefers to use the inclusive pronouns "we" and "us" in connection with positive outcomes in God's grace.

Eighteen lines further on in Ælfric's sermon XIV, he segues into the worst consequences of wrong behavior, but with a significant shift of pronouns. He says "the English people ... who submit to the Danes" (132) betray themselves and their nation in Satan's service, and he notes each traitor will "fall into eternal torments" (138). Ælfric's conscious rhetorical change from the first person plural ("we") in the first passage at lines 98-107 ("But here in the English nation *we* feebly keep the laws God established ... ") to the third person plural in the second passage at lines 126-39 (the implied "they" of "the English people ... who submit to the Danes") is crucial in helping Ælfric achieve his even tone.

The abbot is saying the same thing as the archbishop—those who disobey God will burn in hell—but Ælfric conveys this message obliquely, and his approach could be called Gregorian. As Gregory the Great in *Moralia in Job*, Ælfric often presents traitors as examples for his congregation not to follow. These stories allow him to describe the hellish pain awaiting—certainly not his obedient congregation—but anyone who is disobedient like these exempla.[65]

Ælfric's conclusion to sermon XIV is radiant with divine promises for his congregation:

> "They [Christ's disciples] rowed their heavy ships to shore, and then they abandoned all things to follow Christ." Christ chose fishermen as his followers. They were unlearned men who rejected all things to follow Christ's teaching and Christ himself here in this world. And later they became so very learned the whole Christian faith in Christ's church was raised up through them, with the help of the Savior. To him is glory and honor forever. Amen.

Dorothy Bethurum suggests the contrasting styles of Wulfstan and Ælfric—the one basically trenchant, the other scholarly and poised—may have much to do with their very different clerical lives: Wulfstan was a public figure, an archbishop and a statesman who made laws, while Ælfric was a more private man, a scholar and a teacher (and, one might add, a Benedictine abbot, or *father*).[66] Bethurum compares Wulfstan to Winston Churchill in his brave statesmanship, organizational skills, oratory powers, and leadership qualities, and notes Wulfstan lacked a certain subtlety of mind or interest in philosophical questions.[67] In contrast to the largely moralistic, fiery sermons of this great Anglo-Saxon archbishop and statesman, Ælfric's sermons possess a quiet humanity and a special concern with God's compassion attractive to the anxious modern mind.

---

[65]For examples of Gregory's use of exempla as teaching tools, see Evans, *The Thought of Gregory* (Cambridge: Cambridge University Press, 1986) 72, 137, and Santha Bhattacharji, trans., *Reading the Gospels with Gregory the Great: Homilies on the Gospels, 21-26* (Petersham MA: St. Bede's Publications, 2001) 103. I am indebted to Professor Henry Mayr-Harting for a stimulating discussion of Gregory the Great and Ælfric at the 2003 Sewanee Medieval Symposium.

[66]Bethurum, "Wulfstan," 218. For more information on Wulfstan and his preaching, see Dorothy Bethurum, *The Homilies of Wulfstan* (Oxford: Clarendon Press, 1957) and Roy M. Liuzza, "Religious Prose," in *A Companion to Anglo-Saxon Literature*, ed. Pulsiano and Treharne, 242. Liuzza presents a fresh perspective on Wulfstan, calling his prose "energetic" and pointing out Wulfstan preached "with the conviction of a prophet."

[67]Bethurum, "Wulfstan, " 218.

Translating Old English Sermons into Modern English

Originally I thought to translate these sermons as literally as I could but soon decided against it. Benjamin Thorpe's nineteenth-century translations of the *Catholic Homilies* tend to the literal.[68] Thorpe translates *Halga Gast* as "Holy Ghost," *geworhte* as "wrought," *mede* as "meed" (for "reward"), *þu* as "thou," *weox* as "waxed" (for "grew" or "increased"), *deopness* as "deepness" (for "profundity"), *betwux* as "betwixt," *ungeendod* as "unended," *hæse* as "behest," *getacnode* as "betokened," and *Christes bec* as "Christ's book" (for "Gospel"), diction that would not resonate with twenty-first-century readers. I eliminated obvious archaisms like these and avoided pronouns smacking of antiquity; therefore, the reader will find "you" and "your" for "thou," "thee," and "thine," and the more contemporary "Holy Spirit," for example. I also tried, where possible, both to straighten out the Anglo-Saxon's synthetic syntax and to modernize Ælfric's penchant for ellipsis and hypotaxis, that is, his use of subordinating connectives to stack clause on clause or phrase upon phrase. I often preserved, however, the initial conjunctions characterizing Anglo-Saxon prose.

This translation method is similar to Ælfric's and was first suggested by John Algeo. Both approaches are very traditional, in a sense, and Ælfric is expressing sentiment familiar to classical and patristic minds when he wrote that he translated not "verbum ex verbo" ("word for word"), but "sensum ex sensu" ("according to the sense"). Each time I revised the translations, I tried to make them more palatable to a modern reader. The results show I favored a smooth translation over a literal one, but since this was a very gradual process, occurring over the space of countless slow passes made through the sermons with the Anglo-Saxon texts in hand, I trust whatever literalness I sacrificed to smoothness has not altered their actual message but has instead increased their reading pleasure.

The very nature of translation is a certain necessary interpretation, because the translator must respect the changes history effects on language. That said, my translations are as faithful to the original as I could make them. Still, the Modern-Englishing of these sermons cannot reproduce or

---

[68]Thorpe aimed to give "a conscientiously correct translation, . . . as literal," he said, "as my acquaintance with the language and my notions of good taste permitted." *Homilies*, vii.

even adequately reflect Ælfric's inimitable style, but if they cause the reader some delight or curiosity, they will have proven the act of translation to be that bridge joining two worlds separated by a millennium and joined by one enduring human heart.

Introduction to Sermon I

"The Nativity of the Lord" is a brilliant, severely damaged piece. This Christmas sermon expertly exegeting the complex opening verses of John nearly vanished in the 1731 Cotton fire and survives today "in sadly mutilated form," as Pope notes; but it remains one of Ælfric's best efforts for "careful workmanship, . . . warm and lucid treatment of a difficult theme, and . . . scope." Probably written during Ælfric's Eynsham abbacy, sermon I is a fitting lead for this book of Christocentric Old English sermons.[1]

Sermon I clearly shows Ælfric viewed symbols as no mere representations of objects but as somehow participating in the essence of the objects they symbolized; to this Weltanschauung, symbols *were* what they represented.[2] He understood words and numbers as links between particular phenomena and universal reality; put another way, to this Anglo-Saxon monk, words were not simply useful labels for things, but expressions of ultimate meaning.[3] Therefore, when Ælfric writes about "þæt Word" ("the Word") in his explication of John 1.1., the words themselves—"þæt Word"—are for him an expression of the "Logos" or "Jesus" or "Love" in an immediate, mystical way perhaps lost on the modern mind.[4]

In lines 13-16, Ælfric alludes to the legend of the sharp-eyed eagle. Obviously Ælfric inherited the patristic assignment of man, lion, ox or bull, and eagle for each Gospel writer, from the visions described in Ezekiel 1.10 and Revelation 4.7 (with the eagle representing John, as Ælfric mentions in lines 11-12),[5] but he makes this notion more familiar for his audience by choosing a fascinating Old English allegory to illustrate the special poetic (and potentially ponderous) nature of John's Gospel, which 'sees' the divinity of Christ in a way the other three Gospels do not.

This highly entertaining story was found (in different versions) in the popular medieval source of exempla, the *Physiologus* (or *Naturalist*) (ca. AD 100). This vigilant bird's keen eyes have grown opaque with age, so the old eagle flies up to the sun to burn away this dimness, scorching his wings in some versions, afterwards descending to bathe three times in a fountain, and becoming a new creature. The comparison is that only John was able to look on (and perceive) the Savior's divinity as the unique eagle with his

---

[1] Pope, *Homilies* I.191.
[2] K. J. Woollcombe, "The Biblical Origins and Patristic Development of Typology," in *Essays on Typology* (London: SCM Press Ltd., 1957) 74.
[3] Clemoes, "Chronology," 188.
[4] Pope, *Homilies* I.198 (I.29).
[5] Pope, *Homilies* I.197 (I.13-16).

strong eyes could look on the sun and—not only live—but become rejuvenated. This lively animal tale sometimes concludes with the moral: "So the dimness of the eyes of the heart is healed by the spiritual fountain of the Lord, who is the sun of justice." Ælfric's allusion to this well-known legend of the eagle shows his concern to communicate his exegesis in the best possible way to his Old English audience.[6]

Ælfric begins his verse-by-verse treatment of this Gospel by acknowledging his reliance on the known authority of Augustine, whom he calls at line 55 "that wise and eloquent bishop." In sermon I, as in the others following it in this book, Ælfric especially turns to Augustine (and Bede) for material he then shapes to fit his audience's needs.[7] But Ælfric is also known for his respectful indepedence from his sources, as seen at line five, where he seems to present an independent notion about John's mother (and Zebedee's wife), whom he says is the sister of the Virgin Mary.[8]

Ælfric refers to Hermes Trismegistus at line 110. Pope suggests an Augustinian commentary describing the philosophers attacked by St. Paul in Romans 1.20-22 may hint at this Ælfrician passage.[9] Synonymous with "alchemy" and "magic," Hermes "The Three-Times-Greatest" was regarded as a contemporary of Moses and was often believed to possess divine powers. The *Hermetica* were attributed to him. Ælfric cleverly uses Augustine and a pseudo-Augustinian source here to show the omnipotence of the 'Word' that could make even the heathen Hermes testify about Christ.

Lacunae resulting from the 1731 Cotton fire are indicated in the translation by bracketed asterisks ([* * *]). When possible, these have been completed with intelligent surmises. In this, I relied primarily on Pope's editorial direction as well as my own experience reading Cotton Vitellius C.v. in the British Library, with the technological aid of a Fiber Optic Light Cord (FOLC). FOLC made visible letters and pieces of letters sandwiched

---

[6]Willene B. Clark and Meradith T. McMunn, eds., *Beasts and Birds of the Middle Ages: The Bestiary and Its Legacy* (Philadelphia: University of Pennsylvania Press, 1989) 2; Ann Payne, *Medieval Beasts* (London: The British Library, 1990) 61-63; and Christoph von Steiger and Otto Homburger, eds., *Physiologus Bernensis. Facsimile of the Codex Bongarsianus 318 in Berne's Burger Library* (Basel: Alkuin-Verlag, 1964) 35, 67, folio 10v; cf. Psalm 103.5; Isaiah 40.31.

[7]For more source information on Augustine, Bede, and others, see Pope, *Homilies* I.191-92, 164-68, 195.

[8]See Pope, *Homilies* I.217-20, for a full analysis of this reference and its possible sources.

[9]Pope, *Homilies* I.202.

between modern paper frames probably in 1844 and 1845. The tan onionskin pasting paper used for this restoration obscures thousands of words in the manuscript, rendering them invisible to the naked eye, but not to FOLC. I recovered a few Old English words this way but mostly confirmed the meticulous nature of Pope's 1967–1968 edition of these sermons.[10]

Modern readers accustomed to the flies and lice in Exodus 8.16-24 may be baffled by Ælfric's reference at lines 230 and 233 to the gnats (*gnættas*) afflicting Pharoah. As Pope notes, the Vulgate lists the third and fourth plagues of Egypt as some kind of stinging insect called *sciniphes* (*ciniphes*, *cinifex*) and also several kinds of flies (*muscæ*).[11] Bede's commentary on *Exodus* interprets *cinifex* as a small, stinging, winged insect and adds to the *muscæ* of the fourth plague the *cinomia* or dog fly. Ælfric's *gnættum* and *fleogum* seem to correspond here to the Vulgate's *sciniphes* and *muscæ*, and therefore these 'gnats' are not the 'no-see-ums' of the American South and elsewhere but are to be thought of as stinging midges, blackflies, and sandflies, while Ælfric's *fleogum* indicate something more menacing than the domestic housefly, as anyone who has ever been chased by a black cloud of biting horseflies knows.

---

[10]Carmen Acevedo Butcher, "Recovering Unique Ælfrician Texts Using the Fiber Optic Light Cord (FOLC)," *The Old English Newsletter*, 36.3, December 2003, also referenced online at the *OEN* site, <http://oenewsletter.org/OEN/index.php?file=essays/index.txt>.

[11]This paragraph turns on Pope, *Homilies* I.223.

Sermon I

For the Nativity of the Lord
John 1.1-14

On this feast day of the Lord we read aloud the holy Gospel passage describing the Savior's nativity, and we heard about his divinity and his humanity, as described by John, who lived with him in this world in his household, the son of his mother's sister. And Christ loved him for his pure virginity. And John rested his head on the Savior's breast, within which lived the fountain of wisdom, so he could articulate Christ's divinity accurately. First in Ezekiel and later in Revelation—and by means of spiritual vision—God clearly depicted John as an eagle, and the other evangelists as other creatures. With the penetrating eyes of an eagle, John looked on the Savior's divinity, as the eagle sees the sun's splendor with indefatigable, undamaged eyes, better than all other creatures.

The three other evangelists wrote in their Gospels about Christ's humanity. They described how he came to all people, and they also depicted the miracles he did in this world. Then the bishops in Asia asked holy John to record for them some wisdom concerning the Savior's divinity. And then John asked them for a three-day fast, and after this fast he became so filled with the Holy Spirit that he began to write the holy book of Christ, as follows, *In principio erat verbum, ET RELIQUA*, or, as we translate for you here in the English language: "In the beginning was the Word, and the Word was with God, and the Word was God. This was in the beginning with almighty God. All things were made through the Word, and nothing was made without the Word. That which was made was life in himself, and that life was certainly the light of humanity. And the light shone in the darkness and the darkness didn't comprehend that prophesied light.

"A certain man was sent from God himself to us, and—without a doubt—his name was John. This man came as a witness, to give a true testimony about that light, so all might believe through him. John himself wasn't the light, but he came to tell others about the light. That true Light was Jesus, who enlightens every person who comes into this world born as a human being.

"God was in the world, and this world was made entirely through him, and yet the world didn't know him. God came to his own people, and his own people didn't receive him. To whomever received him, Jesus gave the power to become God's children, to those who believe in his name. They are those who are not born of blood, nor of the will of the flesh, nor of the will of man, but they are born of God. And the Word was made flesh and lived among us. And we ourselves actually saw his glory that is fitting for God's only begotten Son, wholly filled with grace and truth."

Augustine the wise, eloquent bishop said he had heard of no one more ignorant than he himself was about John's holy Gospel because of the profundity of its hidden meaning. However, he did work out some of its meaning with God's help, for God is the source of all understanding. In keeping with Augustine's revelation, we will write this meaning down in English, for the strengthening of your hearts.

The true evangelist, John, said to us with God's help that the Word existed in the beginning with almighty God: "In the beginning was the Word." And that beginning is the Father, and the Word always lived with the Father, and the Word is the beginning, as he said later in John 8.25, *Ego principium qui et loquor uobis*: "I myself am the beginning, even I who am speaking to you." And the great leader Moses had this to say about that beginning, *In principio fecit Deus celum et terram*: "In the beginning God made the heavens and the earth." And that beginning is God's only begotten Son. Through him God created all things and endowed them all with life through the living Spirit. These three are in the beginning and in almighty God.

We speak yet again about that same beginning. The Word was alive in the very beginning with almighty God. And the psalmist sang about the Word in Psalm 33, as we clarify for you here, *Uerbo Domini caeli firmati sunt et spiritu oris eius omnis virtus eorum*: "The heavens were made firm through the holy Word of God, and through the breath of his mouth their power was established." Now here in this little verse the whole holy Trinity is encompassed, for the three-in-one God of heaven is the Father and his Word—who is God's own Wisdom because the Word is the manifestation of Wisdom—and the Holy Spirit, who inhabits all created things. Through the holy Word of the heavenly Father, the holy angels living in heaven are strengthened and made mighty, and through the Holy Spirit they are made to rejoice in the love of their creator, who created them in glory. And the hearts of all people on earth who believe in the one true God are always enlightened through that same Spirit. And by exercising much power, God's Spirit gives all of us forgiveness of our sins.

Then the psalmist sang in Psalm 104, *Quam magnificata sunt opera tua, Domine: omnia in sapientia fecisti; impleta est terra possessione tua*: "O true Lord, your mighty works are greatly magnified, and you made all things in your wisdom, and the earth's sphere is filled with your possessions." In the verse quoted earlier, the Psalmist sang about the Word, and in this one he sings about the Wisdom.

Paul the apostle also wrote in his epistle about Christ our Savior. Paul said Christ was the Wisdom of the holy Father and his wonderful might. Some heathens also said in their writings that we should believe in the true God who rules the heavens and who made all things. One heathen man of old, named Hermes, lived in the land of Egypt before the birth of Christ, and Hermes testified about Christ. The Savior chose this heathen as a witness because of his great wisdom. Hermes wrote one book with the Latin title, *Uerbum Perfectum*, which means in English, *Perfect Word*.

Now we will recount Hermes's words to you truthfully so you can hear how the Wisdom of God enlightened a heathen until he genuinely understood about Christ: *Filius benedicti Dei atque bonae uoluntatis, cuius nomen non potest humano ore narrari. Est autem inenarrabilis sermo sapientiae, sanctus sanctis, de solo Deo: Dominus est omnium, dominante Deo mortalibus, et qui ab hominibus indagari non potest, super omnes est.* He said about our Savior: "He is certainly the Son of the blessed God and of the good will. And no person's mouth can fully articulate his name. He is Wisdom's speech to us unspeakable, and holy to his saints, from God alone. He is Lord of us all, from the ruling God who governs mortals. And he is the one who can in no way be conceived by man and woman because he is above all humanity."

That's what Hermes wrote in his treatise about the almighty Father and his only begotten Son. Hermes called him "Wisdom's speech," and John the Evangelist called him "the Word." And Hermes said that he was from God alone because his divine nature had no mother. He is from God alone, and ineffable to us, as Hermes said. We could tell you many other testimonies spoken by heathen prophets about our heavenly God, if it didn't seem too long to include here.

"In the beginning was the Word, and the Word was with God, and the Word was God. This was in the beginning with almighty God." And some heretics erred in their belief. They refused to believe the living Son of God had always existed with God without beginning. But John the Evangelist refutes such heretics by writing these words: "In the beginning was the Word, and the Word was with God, and the Word was God." From this holy Gospel passage you learn that one is the Father, another is the Son, and third is the Holy Spirit, although common to them all is one divinity always, and one majesty. The one divinity common to them all does not allow them to exist as three gods, nor does it permit any one of them to have less power than the other. And this divinity never began. It was ever dwelling in trinity and in true unity forever.

"All things were made through the Word, and nothing was made without the Word." God's Son was not created, nor is he-through-whom-all-things-were-made a created being. All the created things that you see in this world as well as the unseen, very alive things in heaven, and even the dragons, all of these creatures were created through the true Wisdom who is called the "Word" in John's Gospel. And nothing was made without this Word.

And all these creatures were made with three qualities, *In mensura et numero et pondere*, which in the English language means: "Earlier God established how large they are and how much strength they have and what their length and height are." And God governs them all because God alone is immeasurable.

And no sin and no bad behavior and nothing evil was ever created by God; however, through [* * *] God's will that the angels violated [* * *], and then through Adam in his transgression. Evil has no home. It has no place to live that allows it to exist anywhere except in created things that were created for good. God created the angels for good, and evil was not yet living anywhere; but then they found it and got lost through it. And evil dwells to this day in the miserable spirits and also in those people who turn their minds to meanness and don't stop themselves from being evil. And these spirits trouble and pester good people in various ways. These spirits want to show how much they despise God, so they oppress good people.

God created the heavens as a home for himself and his holy angels who obeyed him, and he also gave this same home to Adam's offspring, if they earned it. But then after Adam's sin, the earth was entrusted to us as our home in this earthly world. And yet God is still good to us. Because of his goodness, God has given us the light of the sun as a lamp during the day, and God also gives us the moon and the stars to light our way at night, and he even gives us various good things to eat. He gives us our food: birds and fishes living in the waters and nourishing wild animals living in the woods. Because of God's great generosity, he has given us all things in common, to the rich and to the poor. Anyone who can catch the animals can eat them.

God also gave us domestic animals and cattle to help us. And he gave us herbs for two reasons—as medicine, and as beauty for the earth. And God gave us cattle as meat, and he also gave us many fruits. We can enjoy all of these according to our needs. And, during our journey of exile on earth, we can earn eternal life with God and a heavenly home if we abandon what is wrong and love our Creator.

Many creatures bother us because of our sins, and they help make us worthy. They help us desire what is best for us. For example, when your colleague says something slanderous about you, in return you naturally take offense because your pride is hurt; however, while you're asleep, you are not even able to protect yourself from fleas and keep them from waking you up. As Moses told us, the Egyptian king who fought against God—Pharoah of old—was so proud that God conquered him with gnats and flies. Moses often interceded for Pharoah and helped Pharoah pray for God's mercy, but the disobedient king still could not flee from the dog's ravenous lice flying into his mouth, nor could he escape the cloud of flies buzzing around his food, nor could Pharoah run from the hum of locusts devouring his fruits. Moses often got mercy for him, but Pharoah swayed the mind of his people against God, until he himself drowned with all of his army in the Red Sea, [* * *] by deceits.

If God had wanted to, he could have very easily sent bears and lions and serpents, even dragons, to fight against the famous king, and in this way he could have upset him. But it was fitting that the insignificant creatures conquered Pharoah's pride, that he [* * *] in the sea. Pharoah would not have perished if he so [* * *].

Often today pieces of money are made out of the earth's gold and silver, but they could not [* * *] be made into pieces of money if God had not first made the ores for them. And we do not own one stick or one staff or one eucharistic wafer for the good of our Mass if God himself hadn't provided it for us at an earlier time; however, we can use God's own things and make him pleased with us. But we can also provoke God if we carry away from him the goodness that belongs to him and that originates in his kind temperament.

In Egypt, clever magicians deceived Pharoah with their magic. Using the same material God created long ago, they performed many pseudo-miracles against Moses, until—overpowered at last—they said: *Digitus Dei est hoc*. They admitted then that "God's finger" was helping Moses, and they could no longer battle him because of the stronger Finger they felt against them.

You can't know more—though we should tell you—of the ineffectual pseudowitchcraft of these Egyptian magicians. But we will say that out of stinking, decaying bull's flesh, bees were born, and—having come alive in this way—they flew around. And out of ass's flesh came wasps, and also out of rotten horse's flesh came hornets. And into each decomposing fruit, came various worms, as we often see ourselves today.

We will now explain the true Gospel further: "That which was made was life in himself." This earth was made, but it in itself is not life; however, the life-giving Reason who created the earth exists in the Wisdom who made the earth. Look at the heavens and sun and moon. They exist in the Strength, we say now more clearly, in the Wisdom of God, who is indeed Life and creates his works according to his temperament. And Jesus is our life in whom we live and move, and in him we exist, as Paul said to us.

"And that life was certainly the light of humanity." Christ is the light of all people who believe in him, as he himself said in John's Gospel, *Ego sum lux mundi, et cetera*: "I am the light of the world, and whoever follows me does not walk in darkness, but has the light of life."

"And the light shone in the darkness, and the darkness did not comprehend that prophesied light." As the sun's light shines upon those who are blind, and they can't see its shining rays, so also the unrighteous and the unbelievers blind in their minds are not able to see the Savior's light illuminating this world.

"A certain man was sent from God himself to us, and—without a doubt—his name was John." John was sent from God to testify concerning the Truth, as his Gospel says later on: "This man came as a witness, to give a true testimony about that light, so all might believe through him." As the daystar at daybreak goes up before the sun, so John shone before Christ's coming. And John baptized Jesus and was also his herald for the holy message.

"He himself was not the light, but he came in order to tell others about the light." The Savior said about John in one place that John was a burning, shining lamp because he boldly told others about Christ. And John the Evangelist says that he himself was not the light because the light of Christ enlightening us all also enlightened John that he was the light.

The Savior also said to his holy apostles, *Vos estis lux mundi*: "You are the light of the world." The Savior said this because the apostles' holy teaching showed humanity the way to faith, as Christ had taught them. Paul also said to the apostles: "Once you were darkness; now you are light in God." Here you can learn that they then believed in the living God. Our eyes are also called lights, but they see nothing without either the light of day or the lights of night.

John the Evangelist also says about the true light: "That true light was he who enlightens every person who comes into this world born as a human being." The true light is our beloved Savior who is himself the light illuminating every person who keeps the light of God's faith in his or her life, either in good nature or in divine wisdom, because all wisdom is from God. And we have not one good thing apart from the grace of God.

"He was in the world, and this world was made entirely through him, yet the world did not know Him." Christ lived in this world divinely, by means of his divinity, and he entered this world through his humanity, by becoming human. And the people who loved this transitory world too greatly would not acknowledge Christ's coming, as John the Evangelist says after this: "He came to his own people, and his own people did not receive him." Instead, they despised and rejected those who believed in Christ. This verse specifically refers to certain people, but many of this world believed in the true Savior, both of the Jewish people and of the Gentiles, though some of them did choose not to believe.

"However many received him, to them all he gave power to become God's children, to those who believe in his name." In these words we can recognize the Savior's generosity and his great goodness towards the children of humanity because—if we believe in him—he gives us power to become God's children. As this Gospel says and as he himself said to some of his chosen ones, *Ego dixi dii estis, et filii Excelsi omnes*: "I told you the truth; you yourselves are gods, and sons of the highest who governs the heavens." What glory and honor this is—that because of his goodness almighty God called us humans gods, and his own children, if we earn the power from him.

On the same subject, God said to Moses earlier, *Ecce constitui te deum Pharaonis; et Aaron frater tuus erit propheta tuus*: "I now appoint you as [* * *] Pharoah's god, and your brother Aaron will be your prophet." So great [* * *] Moses that God appointed him god to the same king who [* * *] fought against the Almighty, but when ten kinds of plagues came to them, [* * *] Red Sea.

The psalmist also sang about this event in the seventh Psalm, *Deus stetit in synagoga deorum: in medio autem deos diiudicat*. He said, "God himself stood in the assembly of the gods, and there he judges between the gods." The Psalmist spoke these words because God himself gives special honor to the people he makes gods, to every one of them individually, as is fitting for them and according to how much they love the living God, he who alone is almighty Creator through himself and in himself always.

And Christ is the only begotten Son of the almighty Father. Because the Savior didn't want to exist as an only child, without brothers and sisters, he came to earth and gathered siblings to himself, so he could reveal his great generosity and give his kingdom to them to reign with him: "They are those who are not born of blood, nor of the will of the flesh, nor of the will of man, but they are born of God." This holy procreation of children is absolutely not of the blood, nor of man's begetting, nor of woman's conceiving. This holy birth is of God's faith.

God himself also said, "Unless a person is born of water and of the Holy Spirit, he or she cannot enter into the kingdom of God." Anything born of flesh is certainly flesh, and anything born of spirit is certainly spirit. These words refer to the spiritual children born of God into God's church through holy baptism and the Holy Spirit, if they persevere in doing good.

"And the Word was made flesh, and it lived among us." The holy Word was not changed into flesh, but the heavenly Prince came here into this world and took up humanity's shape from Mary's womb. He was true man born in soul and body. And yet he remained God in his divinity, one almighty Savior, to redeem us. Those wicked heretics, the Manichees, once said God had dishonored his majesty because he had chosen to be born of woman's nature. But the foolish and the heretic should hear it said that the holy virgin, our Savior's mother, possessed no impurity, not even lust, nor man's company. But the maiden continued to live as a virgin, and she gave birth to her child without experiencing bodily pain.

And because Mary the virgin bore our Lord, it is fitting that she should always be honored in greatness. If, as we often see for ourselves, that the sun shines on foul mud and is not sullied, how much more can the almighty Son of God be born of Mary with no impurity? And she was greatly cleansed through his holy power. So he was not debased, and her virginity remained unblemished, since she bore him without having intercourse.

"And we ourselves actually saw his glory, such glory as is fitting for God's only begotten Son." The apostles who journeyed with him saw the miracles that he did. They witnessed how on one occasion he was transfigured on a certain mountain, [* * *], so their Savior's face shone like sunshine, and his clothes sparkled whiter than snow. Afterwards they saw Christ when he had risen from the dead in a perfect body. And they saw how Christ ascended to heaven, and they observed it [* * *] with great wonder.

John the Baptist baptized the Son of God in the river Jordan, and then Christ went [* * *] up out of the water immediately. And God's voice said from heaven, "This is my beloved Son, who pleases me well." Then later, on the mountain, as we said before, the disciples who were with Jesus when he shone brightly heard the holy Father from heaven saying these words clearly and lovingly: "This is my beloved Son, in whom I am well pleased. Obey him." Matthew said this. Again, on a third occasion, before Christ's passion, the same Father clearly called to him, and everyone following the Savior heard this divine voice. God said that he glorified Jesus, and would continue to glorify him. That God the Father called to Jesus loudly from heaven three times (so people might hear his voice) was certainly a great witness and much glory to the Son; however, some who heard it said it was merely thunder.

The Gospel text for today ends with these words: "Wholly filled with grace and truth." In his humanity Christ possessed so much grace that he was born true God and true man, of David's family, from Mary the pure maiden. One Christ lived in the two natures. He possesses truth, as he himself said, *Ego sum uia, & ueritas, & uita*: "I myself am the way, and the truth, and the life."

Through Moses, both the law of old and public law were established for the people of the Old Testament, but the beloved Savior brought grace and truth to us New Testament people. And Jesus fulfilled the things that were prophesied long ago through Moses and the prophets concerning him. And all the events of his life were planned from the beginning of the world. To God's Son be glory and praise and honor forever with his heavenly Father and with the Holy Spirit in one divinity. We say Amen.

Introduction to Sermon II

The first in a series of sermons for the five consecutive Fridays of Lent, sermon II treats the miracle at the pool of Bethesda in John 5.1-15. The other three sermons translated in *God of Mercy* are III, V, and VI; the fifth is found in Assmann.[1] This series may have been completed by Ælfric even before he finished *Lives of Saints* (998).[2] Ælfric's main source is again Augustine. The details added by Ælfric in lines 10-16 (that the pool was near a temple, the porches built by Solomon and made of "solid hewn stones," and the sacrificial offerings washed in the pool) come from Alcuin's *Commentaria* (and ultimately Eusebius's *Onomasticon*, translated by Jerome) and are also natural inferences made by Ælfric from reading John 10.23, and Acts 3.11, 5.12.[3]

Sermon II provides introductory material about Lent and introduces the major Lenten themes of repentance and healing. However, its harsh words for those who are Jewish presents a problem for modern readers. There is no getting around this point in Old English scholarship. Ælfric writes, "Christ at his coming manifested God's power, and his miracles stirred up the Jewish people into feeling resentment towards his teaching, and they plotted how to betray him (120-24)." Searching through Ælfric's large corpus, a careful reader may note this Anglo-Saxon Benedictine monk utters harsh words—not against all Jews—but towards the "unbelieving" whom he describes as the "Lord's adversaries."[4] Whenever Ælfric is speaking of Jews in conjunction with the persecution and death of Christ, he uses epithets like "unblest," "wicked," "evil," "hardhearted," "presumptuous," "impious," even "bloodthirsty."[5]

But elsewhere Ælfric speaks favorably of Jews, commending them for refusing to eat or drink with Gentiles: "And they were right in doing so. They did not want to become defiled through the foul Gentiles but wanted to practice the true worship of the almighty God in whom they believed."[6] Ælfric preaches that some of the Jews believed in Christ after they had wit-

---

[1] Pope, *Homilies* I.226-29.
[2] Pope, *Homilies* I.226-27.
[3] For a complete explanation, see Pope, *Homilies* I.243, 230-31.
[4] Pope, *Homilies* I.248 (III.3), I.279 (IV.274); I.386 (IX.172-98); and II.538 (XV.167-68); Godden, *The Second Series Text*, 129, 147; and Clemoes, *The First Series Text*, 188, 198.
[5] Pope, *Homilies* I.251 (III.80), I.253 (III.127-28); I.271, (IV.130-31), I.278 (IV.258), I.279 (IV.274); I.344-5 (VII.94-107); II.481 (XII.51-52), II.487 (XII.196); Godden, *The Second Series Text*, 148-49, 128-29.
[6] Pope, *Homilies* I.294 (V.127-29).

nessed his raising of Lazarus and often describes the Church as the amalgamation of the two races—Jews *and* Gentiles who accept Christ.[7] He points out Christ extended his grace to the Gentiles because "in the land of the Jews the Savior did not at all find as many believing people as he wanted to receive heavenly life."[8] These examples show Ælfric was not anti-Semitic. What he condemns is not the Jewish nation or Jewish ethnicity but the rejection by some Jews of Christ. To him, the Christ-rejecting Jews represent all people who refuse to accept and follow the Son of God.

Ælfric most likely knew no Jews; Britain's medieval Jewish community arrived with the Normans in 1066 and was expelled from the country in 1290.[9] John Algeo observes, "For Ælfric, the Jews would have been archetypal embodiments of people who neglect their obligations and are blind to the Truth among them."[10] Like the Christ-rejecting heretics Ælfric often castigates in his sermons, Christ-rejecting Jews give this Anglo-Saxon monk an outlet for vituperative comment. They are one antimodel for his Christian audience. Having contextualized Ælfric's often harsh, sometimes inclusive, always very Old English references to Jews, I still find them disturbing.

Frequent paronomasia helps Ælfric create an encouraging, memorable message. Throughout his sermons, Ælfric refers to Jesus as "Hælend," meaning 'Savior,' and more literally, 'Healer.' He plays on *Hælend*'s Old English root, *hælu* ('health,' 'salvation,' even 'safety') in lines 95-97 to communicate that Christ is both divine defender and doctor: "Hys nama is Hælend, for þan þe he *gehælþ* his folc, / swa swa se engel cwæþ be him, ær þan þe he acenned wære: / He *gehælþ* hys folc fram heora synnum." The translation emphasizes this punning: "Christ's name is *Savior*, because he *heals* his people, as the angel said about him before he was born: 'He *heals*. He will *save* his people from their sins.' "[11] (The modern *hale* meaning 'healthy' has its roots in *hælu*.)

---

[7]For examples, see Pope, *Homilies* I.317 (VI.107-110); I.233 (II.70-75); I.254 (III.142-46); II.517-8 (XIV.53-60).

[8]Pope, *Homilies* II.523 (XIV.182-84) and I.233 (II.68-75).

[9]For more information on this subject, see Patricia Skinner, ed., *Jews in Medieval Britain: Historical, Literary, and Archaeological Perspectives* (Woodbridge: Boydell & Brewer, 2003); H. H. Ben-Sasson, ed., *A History of the Jewish People* (London: Weidenfeld and Nicolson, 1977); and Stephen J. Harris, *Race and Ethnicity in Anglo-Saxon Literature* (New York: Routledge, 2003).

[10]Notes from John Algeo, 10 January 1991.

[11]Pope, *Homilies* I.234 (II.95-97).

Ælfric's discussion of the number forty in this sermon reflects his view that numbers represent ultimate reality. To emphasize the significant relationship between spiritual health and physical acts like good deeds, Ælfric uses numerology to describe the plight and subsequent healing by Christ of the bedridden man. The medieval mind understood forty to represent completeness and obedience.[12] Moses, Elijah, and Jesus all fasted forty days, as the Bible records and Ælfric carefully mentions in lines 151-62.[13] In his explication of Christ's miraculous healing here, Ælfric first discusses the man has been bedridden for thirty-eight years, a number two less than the totality of forty and an indication of this man's fragmented spiritual life, but Ælfric points out that thirty-eight plus the two greatest commands of God give the number forty, or spiritual wholeness. In other words, love God and your neighbor (Matthew 22.37-44; Deuteronomy 6.4-9).

Ælfric also reminds his audience that the community in heaven will be a large gathering limited only by a person's refusal to love God:

> Many people do very often ponder what becomes of all the things and beings that have been created from Adam's time until the present day. But they don't realize the Almighty wants to have a large number of people come into his heavenly kingdom, as is fitting for him, so he may reign in his kind power over a vast crowd. And entirely too many people perish because of their sins. (241-46)[14]

☦ ☦ ☦

---

[12]See Beryl Smalley, *The Study of the Bible in the Middle Ages* (Oxford: Basil Blackwell, 1983) 5.

[13]Pope, *Homilies* I.237.

[14]Pope, *Homilies* I.240 (II.241-46). Also see the introduction to sermon XI for the discussion of a similar inclusive passage.

Sermon II

For the Sixth Day in the First Week of Lent
John 5.1-15

Evvangelium: Erat dies festus Iudaeorum, et reliqua

Dearest people, because biblical teaching will make you more faithful and more dedicated to your Lord, it makes me very happy today to tell you about the holy Gospel passage you heard read aloud a moment ago. John the Evangelist, who was God's darling and the son of Christ's maternal aunt, told the following story about Christ our Savior in his Gospel. On one occasion while Christ was here in this world, living in the flesh, "He really wanted to go to Jerusalem on a certain feast day. In the city near the temple there was a wondrous pool of water called Bethesda. The wise king Solomon had surrounded that pool of water with five colonnades made of solid hewn stones. And there, in the old way, the offerings were washed that were continually presented in Solomon's temple as honor to God, in the Jewish way.

"Through the power of almighty God, miracles regularly occurred in this pool of water because God sent his angel out of heaven's glory, and—at God's command—this angel frequently stirred the water up inside the colonnades. And any unhealthy person stepping into the water after the angel's stirring was immediately healed from whatever infirmity he or she might have had. So on that day in these colonnades there lay many frail people. Their health had been broken in various ways. They were blind or lame or paralyzed in their hands, and they were all waiting for the healing stirring the angel's coming would bring.

"A certain bedridden man had suffered from his illness for thirty-eight winters and lay there, also waiting on the same thing. When the Savior came, as we said earlier, he knew the man had been sick for a long time, so he said to the troubled man, 'Do you want to be made whole?' The man who was crippled answered him, 'But, Sir, I don't have anyone who can put me into the pool of water after the angel's stirring, and when my frail self does finally get there, then someone else steps into the water before me.' Then the Savior said to him, 'Arise whole from that bed. Pick up your sickbed, and walk away from here.' At once, the man was completely healed. He picked up his sickbed and put it on his back and walked away.

"This occurred on a Saturday. The Jews honored that day with festivity, according to Moses's law, and so they said to the man who was healed there: 'It's the holy day of rest. You mustn't move your bedding.' The man answered them with conviction. He didn't hesitate to say, 'The man who healed me commanded me to pick up my bed and walk.' And they began asking him, 'What man commanded you to pick up your bed and walk?' And the man who had been healed didn't know who the Savior was.

"And at that time the Savior left the crowd. Afterwards Christ looked for that man in the temple and gave him this command: 'Look, today you've been healed. From now on, watch yourself. Don't sin, because something worse could happen to you.' And then the man went and told the Jews the Savior had healed him."

We have briefly presented this Gospel, simply and literally, and now we also want to explain its spiritual sense, according to Augustine's interpretation, but briefly, however, because we don't want you to feel burdened. The pool of water was surrounded by five colonnades. As the interpreter points out, this pool signified the Jewish nation, surrounded at that time by the five books of law written by Moses according to God's guidance, so that they should not sin. In the colonnades lay the paralyzed and the sick, the blind and the crippled, and persons with withered hands—like the Jews who were paralyzed in their faith because Moses's law could not make them righteous, until Christ came openly to humanity and put us right by faith and grace, as well as the Jews who believed in him.

People who look the world over but are unable to see the light of faith are blind in their minds; and people who are unkind and fail to fulfill the Savior's commands with works are crippled in their hearts; and people who hear the Lord's commands but won't obey them are deaf. The person who has done no works of mercy has a withered hand, and lives an unfruitful life, and is always shriveled up.

The Savior had this to say about works of mercy, and he said it in his holy Gospel, when a certain lame person lay at the place where the Savior was teaching the people: "Stretch out your hand." And immediately that person became whole when he stretched out his right hand that had been withered until then—as if he were admonished by the mighty miracle. Christ says, "Stretch out your hand" to anyone who has been niggardly in giving gifts of alms for the needy.

So cripples lay inside the colonnades, but the almighty Savior who descended from heaven to redeem humanity was able to heal them in soul and body, through his true grace. Christ's name is "Savior," because he heals his people, as the angel said about him before he was born: "He heals. He will save his people from their sins." That God was willing to be a person in this life and redeem us through himself is a much greater miracle than even the miracles that he worked among humanity while he was here on earth. And the unseen miracles—through which he blotted out the hidden sins of our souls—were better for us than the visible miracles, through which those persons were healed, but later died.

The soul healed from sins and persevering in faith surely goes from this life to God. And the perishable body, though it has been healed, is taken away at death and changed into dust. But it is still healed to perfect salvation afterwards on Judgment Day, when it rises up out of death. After this, it doesn't die, become sick, be hungry or injured by thirst, or grow old. Instead, it's forever eternal afterwards, in soul and in body, free from the fear of death.

At the pool of water were two wonderful powers, one communicated through the angel, and the other through the Savior. After the angel's stirring, whoever could walk into the pool of water was immediately healed from his or her sickness, and whoever came later was unsuccessful because the angel's activities foreshadowed our Savior's coming. Christ at his coming manifested God's power, and his miracles stirred up the Jewish people into feeling resentment towards his teaching, and they plotted how to betray him.

One person was healed after the angel's coming, and the Savior healed one person at his coming, to signify the unity of our faith. And salvation does not come to anyone who exists outside the unity of Christ's church. The water's stirring also prefigured the Savior's suffering. Through Christ's suffering, salvation came to all people who in one faith obey him with holy conduct.

On that day so long ago, Christ healed one person from all those who were sick, and yet he could have easily healed them all with one word. But through that one miracle he wanted instead to awaken their minds and enlighten their souls through the miraculous sign. The bedridden man had remained on his sickbed waiting on health and salvation, thirty-eight winters. Then Christ came, summarizing all holy books in two commands: Love and honor the almighty Lord with faith and all your heart, and then love and honor your neighbor as yourself. Add these two commands to the number that is two less than forty, representing the long sickness of the crippled bedridden man, and then the complete number forty results. The person who does not possess a true love of the Creator and others lives life lacking completeness.

Certainly this number was determined long ago, when Moses fasted forty days and—guided by God—wrote God's law down, and Elijah the prophet fasted just as long. Old Testament prophecy was signified by these events. However, Moses and Elijah were not able to accomplish such fasting by themselves. Omnipotent God gave them the power to do so.

Afterwards then, while our Savior was present on earth, he fasted forty days, through his own strength. This event prefigured the future Gospels that he himself arranged through his four evangelists, as instruction for humanity and as strengthening for their faith. This fast was the origin of our Lent. In this manner, then, Lent was established at an earlier time by God himself, and for that reason we are to keep the holy fast of this season, as our confessor tells us to do.

Now there is also another fast for us to keep, as the apostle Paul wrote about in his epistle. We ought to abstain from sin and from the evil lusts of this world and always live purely, moderately, rightly, and virtuously—waiting for the reward, the blessed hope of our Savior's coming. In doing so, we receive eternal life with him if we now obey his commands with works. And those people who despise him he causes to sink down into the pit of hell.

We fast this fast before Easter with difficulty. And afterwards we live festively fifty days, until the holy Pentecost, when the Holy Spirit came in the likeness of fire and strengthened the faith—first of the apostles, and afterwards, through them, that of all people. In a similar fashion, we should work in this life and rejoice in the future one because of the reward to be received at the eternal festival.

The Savior gave the bedridden man three commands. These were "Arise," "Pick up your sickbed," and "Walk." He healed the man's frailty through his command to him: "Arise." And yet the action also signified something, as if our Savior spoke to the sick man with this meaning: "Immediately shake from yourself the flabbiness of fetid sins in which you lay, and prepare yourself for virtues of the soul."

However, it wasn't enough for the sick, bedridden man to rise up whole. The Savior also commanded him to take his sickbed and walk away. The Savior commanded him, "Pick up your sickbed." This means that—as best you can—be patient and tolerant with your neighbors for their spiteful deeds or ugly words. As the apostle Paul said in an epistle, *Alter alterius onera portate, et sic adimplebitis legem Christi*: "I ask you to bear your burdens among yourselves, and this is how you can be sure to fulfill Christ's law." This includes both love and hate. Every one of us ought to help others with love, and every one of us ought to be merciful towards the evil in our midst, so that God's law will be fulfilled in our community. Above all, Christ's law is true love. It is not fulfilled unless we behave lovingly. We must bear each other's burdens.

Christ also commanded him to "walk." He wanted him to proceed in steps of good works, and not to stand idle. Then the sick man picked up his bed and happily began walking. And the Jews complained because this occurred on a Saturday, which they greatly honored in keeping with Moses's law. This festival began because almighty God created all things, seen and unseen, in six days, and on the seventh day God ceased from his work and hallowed that day. And afterwards God commanded in his law that this day should be kept as a feast because of the secret significance of Christ's suffering, as was known later.

God made all created things and beings in six days, and ceased on the seventh, so from that time on he made nothing else but instead mightily renews these same things among humanity and animals until this very day. He created the first two persons and established all the seasons, but after that he didn't create anything unusual that hadn't been included in the old ordinance he established at the very first. But every day God does create new souls, and he endows them with life in a body, as we learn in books. And the souls aren't created anywhere before God sends them to the created body in their mothers' wombs, and in this manner they become human beings.

You may already know that our souls do not come from our father or mother. The heavenly Father creates the body and quickens it with soul. And God renews all created things continually, the fishes and birds and also four-footed animals, because the former things passed away in old age. And God governs this world with a benevolent purpose, though our evilness may often offend him, and then we suffer difficulties for our sins.

Many people do very often ponder what becomes of all the things and beings that have been created from Adam's time until the present day. But they don't realize the Almighty wants to have a large number of people come into his heavenly kingdom, as is fitting for him, so he may reign in his kind power over a vast crowd. And entirely too many people perish because of their sins.

That same day of rest, as we explained a little earlier, prefigured the day on which our Lord lay dead in the tomb in order to deliver us, at which time he ceased from performing the miracles that he had worked during his life. And on Sunday he rose up out of death, in good health. And ever since that time, Sunday has been hallowed because of the resurrection of our Lord, who was resurrected on that day, and so we celebrate it to honor God. And after that they ceased to celebrate Saturday's festival.

As mentioned earlier, on that earlier day of rest the Jews performed no menial work. And this one day prefigured our entire life. In other words, your life is a spiritual day of rest on which you should always serve God and refrain from sins because these are menial works and cause their workers to be in servitude forever.

The Jews celebrated that day of rest and often lamented when people were healed on that day by our Savior. On one occasion Christ asked them whether or not the terrible suffering of a certain dropsical man might be healed on the feast day they so eagerly honored. Then they all became silent, and the Savior immediately healed the dropsical man as they watched. And afterwards Christ asked them through a parable: "Why, if the ass or ox of any one of you fell into a pit, wouldn't you quickly draw it out on the holy day of rest?" [Luke 14.5] And then they couldn't give him an answer because they'd been overpowered.

Afterwards, the healed man met up with the Savior in the temple, and our Savior said this to him: "Today you've been healed. Guard yourself against sins, so something worse doesn't happen to you." With these words Christ made it clear that the man had been made miserable because of his sins. However, it should be pointed out that not all unhealthy people are afflicted because of their sins, though some are. Some people are made sick so they may become humbler, some are made sick for testing, and some are made sick for God's miracles because God's judgments are very secret. And God is always just in all his actions.

Then, after the healed man had spoken with the Savior, he declared to the Jews that Christ had healed him, and he glorified Christ, praising his power. To whom be glory forever with his almighty Father and with the Holy Spirit in one divinity. Amen.

Introduction to Sermon III

Sermon III is a straightforward, very succinct exegesis of the Parable of the Vineyard/Tenants told by Jesus and recorded in Matthew 21.33-46. As noted in sermon II's introduction, sermons III, V, VI, and II are four in a series of five Lenten sermons perhaps completed by Ælfric even before he finished *Lives of Saints* (998).[1]

Sermon III contains an interesting *hapax legomenon*, the *amberlice* ('cheerfully') found at line 141: "Surely if they [the unbelievers] had known they themselves were being referred to, they would not have answered so *cheerfully*." *Amberlice* is not found in Old English dictionaries, but *ambyre* is (in *ambyrne wind*, 'favorable wind'); this phrase is found in a familiar passage of Alfred's *Orosius*.[2] For *amberlice*, Pope suggests a range of meanings, "useful, helpful, serviceable."[3]

However, I have selected the stronger *cheerfully* for *amberlice* in order to emphasize Ælfric's gentle irony here. Strengthening this choice of diction is the root sense of *ambyr* originating in the combination of *am-*, "even" or "equal," and *-ber*, "let it be," suggesting a certain que-sera-sera insouciance entirely apt at this ironic point in the sermon.[4]

† † †

---

[1] Pope, *Homilies* I.226.
[2] Pope, *Homilies* I.257-58.
[3] Pope, *Homilies* I.258.
[4] T. Northcote Toller, ed., *An Anglo-Saxon Dictionary Based on the Manuscript Collections of the Late Joseph Bosworth*, 1898 (Oxford: Oxford University Press, 1989) 36.

Sermon III

For the Sixth Day in the Second Week of Lent
Matthew 21.33-46

Our Lord often told very dark parables, as when on one occasion he told this parable to his disciples and the unbelieving Jews: "There once was a certain head of a household who commanded a vineyard be built. And he fenced it in and ordered a winepress be dug inside it. And he built a tower, too. And afterwards he let out the vineyard to tenant farmers and went on a long journey to a land far away. Later, when it was nearing harvest time, he sent his servants to the tenant farmers, so they could fetch the fruits of that vineyard. Then the farmers seized the servants of their lord and beat one, killed another, even stoned one to death with stones. Afterwards, that lord again sent other servants, many more this time, and the wicked farmers immediately killed them just as they had killed the others. So next he sent his son to them, saying, 'Surely they will respect my son.' When the tenant farmers saw the son, they said: 'This is the heir. Let's kill him, and then his inheritance will be ours.' And they seized the son and led him out of the vineyard and killed him. 'What, say you, will the lord of the vineyard do to those cruel tenant farmers when he comes to them?' Then the Jews said, 'He will destroy these evil tenant farmers in a terrible manner, and then he will let out his vineyard to others who will give him the fruits at the agreed times.'

"Then the Savior spoke these words to them about the cornerstone: 'Haven't you read in books about that cornerstone, the one the wall builders rejected? Haven't you heard that that stone has been built into the corner of the wall? This has been done by God, and it is wonderful in your eyes. And I tell you that the kingdom of God will for that reason be taken away from you and given to the people who give God fruits. And the person who falls upon that stone will be broken, but the person upon whom that stone falls will be utterly crushed.' When the high priests of the Jews and the Pharisees heard this parable, they immediately recognized he had told it about them, and they discussed among themselves in a secret counsel how they might take Christ by treachery. But they feared the crowd with him at that time because the people considered Jesus a prophet."

We have told you this Gospel text simply. And now we want to reveal its meaning to you because you cannot know all of its hidden meaning unless someone tells you the wise teachers' interpretation of it, as it stands in books. The head of the household who possessed that vineyard is obviously our heavenly God, who had placed the Jewish people in the midst of the best land of this world and established the law for them. As taught in the five books written down for them by Moses, that great leader who led them out of the land of the Egyptians and to that country, the Jews were always supposed to honor only God with their holy worship. And at that time they alone had an understanding of God, and all other peoples served devil-idols.

Through his holy prophets of old, God often called the Jewish people by the name "Vineyard," because they were supposed to produce good fruits for God, as a good vineyard does. About that vineyard the prophet Isaiah wrote: "I expected my vineyard to bear fruits for me, but instead it produced degenerate grapes. Now I will show you what I'm going to do. I will break up its hedge and take it from them, and it will be carried off and its fruits crushed. I will break down its wall, and it will be trodden down. I will lay it waste, and it will not be pruned or dug round; instead, brambles and wild thorns growing in it will damage it. And I will also command the heavenly clouds not to rain one single drop of rain on it. Obviously the vineyard of God is the house of Israel, and I expected them to perform acts of justice, but, look, they only oppress. I expected righteousness, but they only cause anguish." [Isaiah 5.4-7]

God fenced in that vineyard, that is, the people of Israel, with magnificent fortresses and a garrison of angels. The tower God built was the temple made of stone by the wise Solomon in Jerusalem, wondrously crafted to honor God. And that winepress signified the altar inside the temple on which—in the old way—various sacrifices were continually offered to God in faith. God leased that vineyard to the wise scribes and Pharisees who faithfully observed his divine law so they might give him the fruits of good works. And then he went on a long journey abroad.

Many of the people there flourished in God, though some of them were not blessed, and they despised Christ and also betrayed him. Christ chided them, too, saying on one occasion: "Woe to you scribes and Pharisees, you hypocrites who lock up the kingdom of heaven from people, and you yourselves do not go in, nor do you allow in those who wanted to enter. . . . You pay the tithe of your herbs, and yet in truth you neglect the greater commands the law requires of you—right judgment, faith, and works of mercy. These things would surely have been fitting to do, and you should also not neglect the others." [Matthew 23.13, 23]

A little earlier we said that that lord went on a long journey abroad after he had let out his vineyard. However, God does not go far away in any direction because he is the one who makes his presence known in every place. But he did leave that vineyard in their control and let them have their own free will. And God never compelled them in any way because every person has a free will and can choose what to love during his or her own lifetime.

As we said before, the head of that household sent his men to the vineyard, wanting to have his fruits, just as the heavenly God frequently sent patriarchs and prophets to the Jewish people since he wanted to put them right. But the Jews killed some of the prophets and scourged others, as this Gospel text tells us, and they stoned some viciously. Again God sent more servants to the wicked tenant farmers, and they treated them just as they had the others.

At last then, God sent his own Son to them because the almighty God was so merciful to us that he sent his own Son out of heaven to set humanity free, and the wicked Jews were so bold they dared kill him. And this is how Christ redeemed those who believe in him: He never contended against them but was obedient to his Father because of his great love for all people. He voluntarily gave his life for us.

Christ said to the Jews, "What should the head of that household do about the vineyard's tenant farmers?" And they still could not fathom he was referring to them, so they answered, "He will destroy these evil tenant farmers in a terrible manner and then let out his vineyard to others who will give him fruits at the agreed times." They rightly pronounced their own judgment. Surely if they had known they themselves were being referred to, they would not have answered so cheerfully.

Obviously that cornerstone the Savior mentioned as holding the two walls together is the Savior himself, who joined together two peoples to form his church, many from the Jews and more from the Gentiles, creating one congregation in true belief. Because of various sins, many people stumble against that cornerstone, but those who please their Lord by doing penance experience forgiveness. There are two choices then. A person will fall upon that stone, or that stone will fall upon the person. Anyone sinning in Christ is falling upon that stone, and anyone rejecting Christ is the one on whom that stone falls, utterly crushing his or her entire being in eternal torments.

Then Christ said, as we mentioned earlier, "The kingdom of God has been taken away from you and has been given to the people who give him fruits." This means that scriptural wisdom, and all the profundity it speaks about the Lord, has been taken away from them and has been revealed to all who honor God with works and faith.

"When the high priests of the Jews and the Pharisees heard this parable, they immediately recognized he had told it about them, and they discussed among themselves in a secret counsel how they might take him by treachery. But they feared the crowd with him at that time because the people considered him a prophet." Although they recognized Christ as speaking this instructive parable about them, they were still hardhearted and hateful in spirit, not believing in the living Christ. And immediately they became angry and wanted to betray him if they could have figured out how to do so, but they were prevented by the crowd who went with him and heard his teaching and saw his miracles and honored him as a great prophet.

Our faith is greater than that of the crowd because we believe in the living Son of God, that he was always God with his eternal Father and with the Holy Spirit, living in the kingdom of heaven. And God became man because he wanted to, for our deliverance, for which we ever thank him. Let us now gladly contemplate giving God some fruits of good works. And may we always honor him with our faith so we may have eternal life with the Savior, as he promised those who love him.

To Christ be glory and praise forever. Amen.

Introduction to Sermon IV

Sermon IV exegetes the exorcism by Jesus recorded in Luke 11.14-28 and Matthew 12.22-30. Pope suggests IV is "roughly contemporary" with Ælfric's *Lives of Saints* (998); it may have been written almost contemporaneously with sermons II, III, V, and VI.[1] Bede's commentary, *In Lucæ Evangelium Expositio*, is the principal source here.[2]

Sermon IV shows Ælfric's keen interest in etymology and definitions (or name interpretations), evident in many of his sermons.[3] In lines 76-85, Ælfric defines *Beezelbub* to make this odd name more familiar to the Anglo-Saxon audience,[4] and in lines 105-106, he uses the Old English *comitatus* topos to make his explication of Luke 11.17 uniquely memorable: "And if the lord of a band of warriors commands his young men and is attacked by them, his comitatus immediately becomes divided."[5] Because the loyalty between lord and retainer was historically the supreme bond in Anglo-Saxon culture, Ælfric's peculiarly English explanation of this Lukan verse intimately articulated for his congregation the thrust of Christ's words about the destructive nature of division: "Every kingdom divided against itself goes to ruin, and a divided household falls" (Luke 11.17 NEB).

In this sermon, Ælfric also treats the familiar medieval topos of the harrowing of hell, that popular medieval legend derived from the pseudepigraphical Gospel of Nicodemus (AD 300–500).[6] He uses this topos as a way of praising Christ as God's champion, the victorious warrior leader able to descend into very hell to rescue Adam and his descendants:

> Satan is the strongman our Lord is speaking of, for at that time Satan had the world in his power because of Adam's transgression. But the Son of God came, stronger than Satan, and conquered him—carried off his weapons, shattered his stratagems, divided his spoil—which Christ redeemed with his death when he took Adam and Eve and their offspring, a great number of people, away from the wicked devil, and led them out of hell up to the kingdom of heaven.[7]

---

[1] Pope, *Homilies* I.260.
[2] Pope, *Homilies* I.259.
[3] See also "De Initio Creaturæ" in the first *Catholic Homilies* series, where Ælfric explains that *Lucifer* means "Leohtberend" ("Lightbearer") and "Aeua" ("Eve") means "lif" ("life"); Clemoes, *The First Series Text*, 179, 182.
[4] Pope, *Homilies* I.268-69 (IV.76-85).
[5] Pope, *Homilies* I.270 (IV.105-106).
[6] William H. Hulme, ed., *The Middle-English Harrowing of Hell and Gospel of Nicodemus*, EETS Extra Series 100 (c) (London: Kegan Paul, Trench, Trübner & Co., 1907) lx-lxx; cf. Isaiah 42.7, 45.2, 53.8-9; 1 Peter 3.19, 4.6.
[7] Pope, *Homilies* I.274-5 (IV.188-96); cf. I.348 (VII.181-86).

Although Ælfric is giving the standard patristic interpretation here of Matthew 12.29 (cf. Luke 11.21-22), he knew the martial description was especially appropriate for his audience, dependent as Anglo-Saxon society originally was on the loyalty of each warrior in the comitatus to his lord or "ring-giver."

At lines 249-51, Ælfric lists the eight deadly sins as "gluttony, promiscuity, greed, anger, laziness, gloominess, and narcissism. And the eighth is pride." Bede only referred to seven sins, without naming them, and when Haymo revised and expanded Bede, he also listed seven sins, following the order in the pseudo-Alcuin *De Octo Vitiis Principalibus* and giving pride of place to *superbia*, while omitting *accidia* (*asolcennyss*, 'laziness'). Ælfric, however, includes 'laziness' (*asolcennyss*) here and saves *superbia* (*modignyss*) for last.[8]

Sometimes Ælfric's etymological bent leads to paronomasia, as in lines 289-92, where he uses it to describe the profundity of the church as spiritual mother. Ælfric plays off the Old English feminine pronoun *heo*, which can refer to both Mary and the feminine noun, *Gelaþung*, or "Christian church" (mentioned by Ælfric previously in line 283): "Eadig is Maria þæt arwyrðe mæden, / þæt heo Godes Sunu abær bliðe to mannum; / ac *heo* is swaþeah git swyþor eadig, / for ðan ðe *heo* Godes word lufað and healt" ("Blessed is Mary the venerable virgin because she happily bore God's Son as man, but nevertheless *she* [or *it*, referring to the church] will still be more abundantly blessed because *she* [or *it*, referring to the church] loves God's word and keeps it").[9] The translation in the text suggests this complex paronomasiatic meaning: "Blessed is Mary the venerable virgin because she happily bore God's Son as man, but nevertheless she—and we—will still be more abundantly blessed because we love God's word and keep it."

† † †

---

[8] Pope, *Homilies* I.284.

[9] Pope, *Homilies* I.280 (IV.289-92). For more information on Ælfric's word play, see Pope, *Homilies* I.131-32, and Joyce Hill, "Ælfric's Use of Etymologies," in *Old English Prose: Basic Readings*, ed. Paul E. Szarmach (New York: Garland Publishing, 2000) 316. Another classic example of this monk's paronomasia is found in the first series of *Catholic Homilies* and involves the Old English word *hlaf* for 'bread': "*Bethleem* is gereht 'Hlaf-hus,' and on hire wæs Crist, se soða hlaf, acenned" ("*Bethlehem* means 'Bread-house,' and in Bethlehem, Christ, the true bread, was born"; see Clemoes, *The First Series Text*, 192.

Sermon IV

For the Third Sunday in Lent
Luke 11.14-28; Matthew 12.22-30

During that glorious time when the merciful Savior lived with us in true humanity and worked miracles, an insane man was brought to him, strangely tormented. His sight and speech had in fact been taken from him. He was left dumb and blind and mad in the most evil fashion. And then the merciful Christ by his divine power healed that man and exorcised from him the evil devil tormenting him all that time. Sane then, this man could speak and hear well, and the crowd were astonished. Then the Jews accused our Lord of working miracles by the power of the devil men call Beelzebub, but they were completely lying.

Some also wanted Jesus to show them a strange sign from heaven, but when he perceived their conniving thoughts, he told them: "Every kingdom divided against itself is absolutely destroyed and does not dwell in peace, and household falls upon household. If the evil spirit is really divided against itself, how then can the evil kingdom stay unified? You say I have driven devils out of people by the power of the devil men call Beelzebub, but if in his name I drive devils out of others, then in whose name do your sons drive them out?" [Luke 11.17-19; Matthew 12.25-27] The Savior said this about his apostles, who were their sons and relatives, and in their Lord's name they exorcised devils and worked many miracles in the sight of the people.

Then the Savior said to the hardhearted people: "Surely if I put devils to flight by the finger of God, the kingdom of God is absolutely come among you. When a strong man guards his hall securely, then the things he owns exist in peace. But if a stronger man comes and overpowers him, then the stronger person wins all the weapons in which his opponent had trusted, and divides his spoil.

"The person who is not with me is against me, and the person who does not gather with me scatters. When an unclean spirit goes out of someone, the spirit wanders through waterless places seeking rest, but in reality does not find it. Then the foul spirit says he wants to go back into the house he went out of. And when he arrives there, he finds it put in order. Then he invites seven other spirits worse than he is, and they go live in that person. And the condition of the person they inhabit is worse than it had been earlier." [Luke 11.20-26; Matthew 12.28-30, 43-45]

When Jesus had said this, a woman in the crowd said to him with a loud voice, "Blessed is the womb that bore you as man, and happy are the breasts you sucked." The Savior answered her, "Still more blessed are those who hear God's word and keep it."

We gather the meaning for this Gospel text from the two evangelists, Luke and Matthew, and we want to tell you its significance briefly. By his heavenly power our Lord healed that poor madman from his madness and from the muteness resulting from his fiendish bonds and from the blindness the devil blinded him with. And the crowd was astonished.

Daily the Lord works the same wonders for us, in a spiritual sense. Within God's church, the Lord truly converts sinful people. When the unbelieving person who previously wallowed in sins submits to the Lord with true penance and forsakes the misleading devil, he or she is cleansed from the unclean spirit and has the light of faith and praises the Lord.

"Then the Jews alleged that our Lord must work miracles in the name of the devil whom men call Beelzebub, but they were completely lying." Once before we spoke of this disgraceful devil. The heathen peoples believed in him. Some called him "Beel," others "Báál." And this devil had the evil surname, "Zebub," referring to the shameful offering heathens offered to him as if to a highly honored god: they killed sheep and oxen and offered them to him, and then flies nested near the foul offering. So his worshippers called him *Beelzebub*, meaning, "Lord of the Flies," or "he who has flies," because *zebub* means "fly." The Jews insulted the Lord when they said he must drive devils out from people in the name of the god who is a cruel devil and has no power to heal others.

"Some of them also wanted him to show them some strange sign from heaven," but they said this to tempt him. The Jews had seen clear signs in the mad man who had been healed there, and yet they wanted to see miracles from above out of heaven, testing Christ because of their unbelief. But Christ said to them when he saw their conniving thoughts: "Every kingdom divided against itself is absolutely destroyed and does not live in peace, and household falls upon household." If a worldly king fights against his people and the people then rebel against their royal lord, this contention will result in their destruction; and in this manner the kingdom will be quickly destroyed. And if the lord of a band of warriors commands his young men and is attacked by them, his comitatus immediately becomes divided.

Then the Savior spoke these words to them about the hostile devil: "If the evil spirit is really divided against itself, how then can his kingdom stay unified?" No devil is ever willing to drive out another. Instead, with one mind they all scheme, devising stratagems for how they may deceive people and lead them to hellish torments, to the place where they themselves live. And their kingdom is in the fierce punishments after Doomsday forever.

"You say I have driven devils out of people by the power of the devil called Beelzebub, and if in his name I drive devils out of others, then in whose name do your sons drive them out?" The Savior said this about his apostles who were their sons and relatives, and in the name of their Lord they drove devils out and worked many miracles in the people's sight. *Ideo ipsi iudices uestri erunt*: "Therefore, these same men will be your judges afterwards." The holy apostles who followed the Savior's true teaching were destined afterwards, on that great day of judgment, to be the judges of all people, both of the Jews and of other peoples, even though they themselves came from the evil nation that rejected Christ and also killed him.

Then the Savior said to that hardhearted people, "Surely if I put devils to flight by means of the finger of God, the kingdom of God is come among you." "The finger of God" in truth signified the Holy Spirit, as Matthew wrote down, saying with these words, *Si in spiritu Dei eicio demones*: "If by the Spirit of God I drive devils out." This finger totally overpowered the magicians in the land of the Egyptians in the presence of Pharoah, when they struggled against Moses and against God and wanted to create gnats, but God did not let them. Overpowered then, they admitted, *Digitus Dei est hoc*: "This is the finger of God."

This same finger wrote Moses's tablets on the mountain called Sinai. On the tablets ten commandments were written down. This is the old law, intended as guidance for all people, both for those of ancient days and for us who live in this world now.

"The hand of God" is without a doubt Christ our Savior, through whom God created all things. And "the finger of God" is certainly the Holy Spirit, through whom our Lord drove out the devils, and through whom all living creatures are quickened with life, and through whom the holy Father distributes among his saints various gifts and much power, and through whom all prophets prophesied about Christ. For us there is no other limb so well adapted for every work as our fingers, and for that reason the Holy Spirit is called "God's finger" because of the many gifts God gives his saints through the Holy Spirit, to every person as needed.

Nor shall any person imagine that—because Christ is called "God's hand" in books—our Savior possesses less heavenly power than his Father.

No, Christ is God Almighty, and the Holy Spirit in heavenly glory is always almighty God in one godhead with the holy Father and Christ the Savior, these three one almighty God ever reigning. And their kingdom is never divided, never destroyed, but remains forever.

Profecto peruenit in uos regnum Dei: "Surely God's kingdom is come among you." Christ himself is God's kingdom, as he said in another place, *Regnum Dei intra uos est*. In English that means, "The kingdom of God is among you." God's kingdom is also God's church, which is all Christian people who believe in Christ. And Christ also brings them to the heavenly kingdom, and those he brings there come both from the Jewish people who have believed in Christ, and also from other peoples who faithfully keep his faith.

"When a strong man guards his hall securely, the things he owns exist in peace. But if some stronger man comes and overpowers him, the stronger one wins all the weapons in which his opponent had trusted, and divides his spoil." Satan is the strong man our Lord is speaking of, for at that time Satan had the world in his power because of Adam's transgression. But the Son of God came, stronger than Satan, and conquered him—carried off his weapons, shattered his stratagems, divided his spoil—which Christ redeemed with his death when he took Adam and Eve and their offspring, a great number of people, away from the wicked devil, and led them out of hell up to the kingdom of heaven.

Qui non est mecum aduersum me est: "The person who is not with me is against me, and the person who does not gather with me scatters." Our Lord's deeds and the devil's cannot be reconciled in any way, nor are they in any way similar because the Savior always wants to save us, and the devil desires our ruin. Christ always draws us to virtues, and Satan to evil deeds. But we must always obey our Lord and Shepherd, and not the hateful wolf, who is intent on this one thing—how with various sins he can separate us from our merciful Savior. And wicked people who wrongly persuade others to do devilish works contend against Christ. They do not gather with him, but scatter souls instead.

"When an unclean spirit goes out of someone, the spirit wanders through waterless places seeking rest" but instead finds no agreeable home in those who are pure in heart. This spirit abandons people with pure hearts and minds serving Christ because in their purity they are "waterless." And he seeks rest for himself in reckless people who live redundant, foul lives, as our Lord said concerning the devil: *Sub umbra, inquit, dormit in secreto calami, et locis humentibus*. In our English language that means, "He rests himself in shadow, in the hiding place of the reed, and in damp places." The devil rests in dark shadows because he sleeps in the black intentions that are not found in the lives of those who are the lights of faith. And he always makes his home in people who are sweaty from stinking lust, as well as in those whose hypocrisy makes them hollow as reeds, outwardly shining but inwardly empty.

The devil is driven out from a heathen person through the power of our Lord when a person is baptized. Then the devil seeks a home for himself everywhere, but he does not find an agreeable home for himself in those who are pure. "Then the foul spirit says he wants to go back into the house he had left," and even into a Christian person if he or she does not faithfully observe good Christian behavior, as God commands. Every person must reject the devil's deeds and arrogance.

"The evil spirit then comes to his old home and finds it swept and empty and all put in order for him." A person is cleansed from unclean sins through holy baptism administered in the Savior's name. But if after baptism this person has no good works, he or she wears the devil's soiled garment of hypocrisy, and "then that evil spirit takes to himself seven other spirits worse than he; and they go live in that person. And that person's life is worse than before."

The seven spirits are the seven capital sins. These are gluttony, promiscuity, greed, anger, laziness, gloominess, and narcissism. And the eighth is pride. If the capital sins are alive in a person, God's Spirit has no home there. Instead, that person belongs heart and soul to the devil if they were to die in that sinful state. It would have been infinitely better if that person had never known the way of truth, than that he or she should turn from the truth to the black devil.

The Savior said to the hardhearted Jews, *Sic erit et generationi huic pessime*: "This will surely happen to this worst of generations." When the Jewish people received God's law, the terrible spirit left them. But then they rejected Christ, put him to death, and cast off God's law that prophesied about Christ, and this evil spirit returned with the seven capital sins. Then their condition became worse than it had been before because they rejected the true Savior, our Redeemer, and accused him in various ways.

When Christ had said this, a woman in the crowd said to him with a loud voice, "Blessed is the womb that bore you as man, and happy are the breasts you sucked." Through this woman's voice, the impious Jews—the Lord's adversaries—were shamed, and their faithlessness was revealed through her faith. Also, her true faith helped her overcome all the heretics who erred concerning Christ. These heretics said Christ had not existed in true humanity, but this woman knew Mary's womb was absolutely blessed by bearing God's Son, and she knew that the breasts Christ sucked in his childhood were happy. The words and steady faith of this woman undoubtedly prefigured God's church, which is all Christian people who now believe in Christ and who in true faith praise the faithful Savior both with their minds and with their mouths.

The Savior answered her, "Still more blessed are those who hear God's word and keep it." Blessed is Mary the venerable virgin because she happily bore God's Son as man, but nevertheless she—and we—will still be more abundantly blessed because we love God's word and keep it. Blessed are all those who hear the holy word of God and keep it with love.

Let us praise our Lord and also love the holy Word of God and keep it with faith. The Almighty Ruler grant us this, he who reigns forever. Amen.

Introduction to Sermon V

Sermon V uses dramatic dialogue to tell the story of the Samaritan woman at Jacob's well, in John 4.5-42. An Augustinian commentary is the principal source for Ælfric's interpretation.[1] As noted earlier, this sermon is one in a series of five Lenten sermons completed by Ælfric before he finished *Lives of Saints* (998).[2]

In a characteristic move away from the negative, Ælfric chooses not to treat the verses dealing with the Samaritan woman's many husbands, focusing instead on two simple Lenten themes in his interpretation of the pericope:[3] Christ's universal offer of salvation and each person's need for humility. God's universal offer of salvation is symbolized, Ælfric notes, in the meeting between the Son of God and the Samaritan woman, a bonafide outsider, the type of all Gentiles who would believe in Christ through humility. An extended passage on humility (lines 174ff.) underscores this very Benedictine concern:

> Today we do not need to climb with difficulty up steep mountains in order to worship, as if God could be nearer to us on a high mountain rather than down in a deep valley. The lofty mountain signifies elevated pride, and the valley symbolizes humility, which our Lord loves. And we ought to worship with true humility if we want our heavenly God to hear us because God is the one who lives in a high place and yet has regard for the deep down humble, and God is always near to those who sincerely call to him in their trouble.[4]

Ælfric also points out the central paradox in Christianity—Christ's human weariness did in no way lessen his divinity (lines 101-12):

> The Savior was weary, though it is wondrous that he was. Through him his heavenly Father made all created things without labor. Neither the Father nor the Son labored at all in that great work, but Christ still became weary in his humanity, after the nature of man. And Christ's weakness is our strength because his strength created us, and his weakness redeemed us. At the sixth hour Christ sat weary at the well, and at the sixth age of this world he came to earth to redeem humanity.[5]

In this quotation Ælfric compares "the sixth hour" of a weary Christ to the world's "sixth age," showing the Old English proclivity for pattern finding. God's six-day act of creation was transferred by patristic fathers

---

[1] Pope, *Homilies* I.286.
[2] Pope, *Homilies* I.226. The other three in *God of Mercy* are II, III, and VI.
[3] Pope, *Homilies* I.286.
[4] Pope, *Homilies* I.296 (V.174ff.).
[5] Pope, *Homilies* I.293 (V.101-12).

(taking their cues from Jewish rabbis) to a six-phased world history, with the sixth age beginning when Christ came to earth and lasting until his Second Coming return. Patterns were also created by the typological relationship of Old and New Testament events and by extrapolating Old Testament events to construct new meanings.[6]

Ælfric's love of definition is seen at lines 208-13: "*Messiah* in Hebrew, *Christ* in Greek, *Unctus* in Latin, is 'anointed' in English—that is, our Savior, who was mightily anointed in his humanity by the Holy Spirit with the seven gifts, as the prophet Isaiah said to us in the prophecy he wrote about Christ."[7] The seven gifts of the Spirit are also a recurring Ælfrician theme.[8]

† † †

---

[6]Clemoes, "Chronology," 189.
[7]Pope, *Homilies* I.297 (V.208-13).
[8]For examples, see Pope, *Homilies* I.384-85 (IX.121-49); I.418 (XI.68); and II.121-23 (XVII.572).

Sermon V

For the Sixth Day in the Third Week of Lent
John 4.5-42

In this Gospel text John the Evangelist said, "While Christ our Lord was in this world, on one occasion he came to a city of Samaria, to the field of the patriarch called Jacob, who had given that field to his son Joseph. And the well Jacob made was there. Then the Savior sat down beside the well, weary from his journey. Because it was midday, his disciples went into the city to buy food for him. And he waited there a while. In the meantime, a certain woman came out of the city of Samaria to that watering place, wanting to draw water.

"And the Savior said to her, 'Give me something to drink.' The woman answered him: 'What makes you ask me this? You are Jewish, and I am a Samaritan woman. The Jews are not willing to eat or drink with Samaritans.'

"The Savior answered her, 'If you had recognized the gift of God and had known who said to you, "Give me something to drink," most likely you would have asked God to give you some of the living water, and he would have.'

"Then the woman said to him: 'This well is deep, and you don't have a pitcher for drawing water. Where will you get living water from? Are you saying you are greater than our father Jacob, who gave us this well? And he himself drank from it, and his children and animals.'

"The Savior answered her: 'Every person who drinks this water will thirst again, but those who drink the water I give them will not thirst in eternity. In them this water becomes a true spring of water rushing towards eternal life.'

"The woman answered him, 'Lord, give me some of this living water so that from now on I will never thirst, nor will I ever need to draw water from here again.'

"The Savior said to her, 'Go call your husband and then come back.' She answered him, 'I don't have a husband.' The Savior said: 'You answered well, woman, when you said, 'I don't have a husband.' You had five husbands, and the man you now live with is not your husband. You told the truth when you said that.'

"Then the woman said: 'Lord, I see you are a prophet. Our fathers used to pray on this mountain, and yet you Jews say Jerusalem is the place where prayers should be said.' The Savior answered her, 'Believe me, woman, the time is coming when you won't pray to the heavenly Father on this mountain or in Jerusalem because you Samaritans worship that which you do not know. We worship that which we know because salvation is from the Jewish people. But the time is coming, and is now here, when true petitioners will pray to the Father in spirit and truth. And God the Father seeks such petitioners who will pray to him. God indeed is spirit, and those who pray to him must worship him in spirit and in truth.' Then the woman said to him, 'I know that he who is called the Messiah—that is, Jesus Christ—will come to us, and when he comes, he will tell us all things.' The Savior answered her, 'I am he who speaks to you.'

"Then Christ's disciples returned and were astonished to see him speaking to this woman, but none of them dared ask what she wanted with him or what Jesus had said to her. Then the woman left her water pot there and went into the city, and said to its inhabitants: 'Come and see with your own eyes the man who has told me all the things I have ever done. Sirs, tell me whether he himself could be the Christ.' And the residents rushed out to Jesus.

"Meanwhile, Jesus's disciples begged him, 'Eat, dear teacher.' And he answered them with these words, 'I have food to eat that you don't know of.' Then his disciples discussed this secretly, wondering whether anyone had brought him any food there. The Savior then said to them, 'My food is strictly that I work the will of the One who sent me here and finish his work.

"'Don't you have a saying that "there are yet four months before the harvest comes"? But I say to you, look at the lands because they are ready for harvest now. And the person who reaps that harvest is receiving a reward, and that person gathers fruit into eternal life, so that the person who sows and the person who reaps may rejoice together. This is a true saying. One person sows and the other person reaps. I send you to reap that which you did not sow. Others labored on it, and you have gone out into their labors.'

"Many of the people of Samaria believed in the living Savior because of the testimony of that woman. She said he had told her all the things she had ever done. When the city's residents came to Jesus, they begged him to stay longer. And so he stayed there two days. And many more believed because of his wonderful teaching, and then they said to the woman: 'We do not believe because of your words now, for we ourselves heard and absolutely know this is truly the Savior of the world.'"

A lengthy interpretation belongs to this Gospel passage, but you cannot understand all of its depth unless it is told to you briefly, for its profundity might trouble you greatly. The Savior was weary, though it is wondrous that he was. Through him his heavenly Father made all created things without labor. Neither the Father nor the Son labored at all in that great work, but Christ still became weary in his humanity, after the nature of man. And Christ's weakness is our strength because his strength created us, and his weakness redeemed us. At the sixth hour Christ sat weary at the well, and at the sixth age of this world he came to earth to redeem humanity.

As we said to you earlier, a Samaritan woman came to the Savior, and because she was foreign to the Jewish race, she was a type of all the church that now believes in Christ, which is made up of all peoples who submit to God's Son in faith. As you have heard, the Savior asked the Samaritan woman for something to drink. He asked her this because he desired faith for her. He wanted her to believe in him and renounce the heresy of devil worship, since Samaritans revered heathen gods then.

But the woman wondered why he wanted to drink from her drinking vessel because the Jews would never eat anything with the Gentiles, nor would they drink from their drinking vessels. And they were right in doing so, for they did not want to become corrupted through contact with unclean Gentiles. They wanted to practice the true worship of the almighty God.

Christ said to the woman, "If you had recognized the gift of God." God's gift is the Holy Spirit. God gives this Spirit to his chosen ones, and his Spirit lives in them and directs them always to the will of God and to good works. That is the water he promised to the woman.

And Jesus said this about the water in the well: "Every person who drinks this water thirsts again, but those who drink of the water I give them will not thirst in eternity. But in them it becomes a spring of water rushing towards eternal life."

And that is in fact what our Lord said before his passion: "Everyone who thirsts should come to me and drink. Whoever believes in me, as scriptures say, 'From his belly will flow a stream of living water.'" The Savior said this concerning the Holy Spirit, who was received by those who believed in him. His Spirit is the living Spring, and those in whom God's Spirit lives do not thirst in eternity but are given eternal life in the heavenly kingdom.

That woman did not yet know what sort of water Jesus meant, and so she said, "Lord, give me some of this living water to drink, so that from now on I will not thirst, nor will I ever need to draw water from here again." She wanted even then to be without labor, but she had not yet heard what the Savior had said to his apostles in another other place: "Come to me, all who labor and are burdened, and I will refresh you."

You cannot understand the great depth of this Gospel text, as we said before, and so we will shorten this explanation quite a bit. Jesus said to the woman: "Believe me, woman, the time is coming when you will not pray to the heavenly Father on this mountain or in Jerusalem because you Samaritans worship that which you do not know. We worship that which we know because salvation is from the Jewish people. But the time is coming, and is in fact here, when true petitioners will pray to the Father in spirit and truth. And God the Father seeks such petitioners who will pray to him. God indeed is spirit, and those who pray to him must worship him in spirit and in truth."

Today we do not need to climb with difficulty up steep mountains in order to worship, as if God could be nearer to us on a high mountain rather than down in a deep valley. The lofty mountain signifies elevated pride, and the valley symbolizes humility, which our Lord loves. And we ought to worship with true humility if we want our heavenly God to hear us because God is the one who lives in a high place and yet has regard for the deep down humble, and God is always near to those who sincerely call to him in their trouble. Nor do we ever have to wander far and wide seeking our benevolent God. Those who always enjoy the indwelling presence of God's merciful Mind do not have to do this. And God is always present in everyone who does good deeds in every land where his faith exists.

The Jews who worshipped God prayed to him in the temple, and Christ said to the woman, "We worship that which we know because salvation is from the Jewish people." That salvation is Christ our Savior, who came from the Jewish race out of Mary, who was of the royal family and bore the King of heaven and earth as our redemption. The prophets who prophesied that it was to come knew this. From that race came Christ's apostles and many others who after his resurrection sold their possessions and placed everything at the feet of the apostles. And they followed Christ without greed, and the apostles shared their food among themeselves equally.

The woman said to Christ, "I know the Messiah is coming, who is called Christ." And he told her, "I am he who speaks to you." And then his disciples returned. *Messiah* in Hebrew, *Christ* in Greek, *Unctus* in Latin, is "anointed" in English—that is our Savior, who was mightily anointed in his humanity by the Holy Spirit with the seven gifts, as the prophet Isaiah said to us in the prophecy he wrote about Christ [Isaiah 11.1-3 LXX].

"Immediately, the woman left her water pot there, and hurried to the city and told everyone about Christ." When she heard from the mouth of the Savior, "I am he who speaks to you," then she rushed home to the city and began to tell everyone there about Christ. She left her water pot, which had the significance of worldly desire, and she became Christ's herald, declaring the truth to the residents of the city. And many believed on the living Savior through that woman's testimony.

"Meanwhile, his disciples begged him, 'Eat, dear teacher.' And he answered them, 'I have food to eat that you do not know of.'" Here we can learn that our Savior ate, since his disciples invited him to have some food, even though a certain Mass priest—whom we will not accuse—may heretically deny that our Lord ever ate in this world. Indeed, this Mass priest was not telling the truth. He did not know then the book of Christ telling us our Lord ate just as other people do, both before his passion and after his resurrection. Christ really ate and drank because he was true man. He ate without gluttony and drank without drunkenness, and he lived all his life without sinning. He had not one vice.

Jesus said, "My food is that I work the will of the One who sent me here and fulfill his work." Christ's spiritual food is the redemption of humanity. And Jesus thirsted for the woman to have faith in him, and he always desires the salvation of our souls. And at that time he worked the will of his Father when he converted the residents of that Samaritan city to faith.

Jesus said: "I say to you, look at the lands, because they are ready for harvest now. And the person who reaps that harvest is receiving a reward, and that person gathers fruit into eternal life, so that the person who sows and the person who reaps may rejoice together. This is a true saying. One person sows and the other person reaps. I send you to reap that for which you did not sow. Others labored on it, and you have gone out into their labors."

The patriarchs and the prophets who proclaimed the Savior were the sowers who sowed God's teaching. And those who then believed in God were certainly the harvest Christ spoke of. And the apostles were obviously reapers who gathered the harvest into God's barn (that is the heavenly kingdom), where they are kept safe, so that in eternal bliss the sowers and the reapers may rejoice together over their labor. Our Savior sowed the Gospel faith among his people through his own self then and also later through his apostles and their successors.

And that seed now grows until the end of this world, mingled with weeds. Weeds are the wicked who live among the Christians here in this world. Angels are the reapers at the end of time, as Christ himself said in some of his Gospels. Angels separately gather the sinful people and those who did wicked things in their lives, and hurl them, bound, into the burning fire, where there is weeping and wailing forever. Then the righteous shine, as the Son does now, in their Father's kingdom. The Savior said this.

The city's residents believed, as we said before, first through that woman's testimony, and later, when they came to where Christ sat, they asked him to stay longer. And he did just that, staying there two days, teaching the people until they believed fully. And they said to the woman who had told them about him before: "We do not now believe through your testimony. We ourselves heard and know as truth that this is really the Savior of the world." In him we also believe, he who redeemed us. To God be glory and praise forever. Amen.

Introduction to Sermon VI

Sermon VI is a powerful call to repentance. It treats the miraculous raising of Lazarus pericope, John 11.1-45. Ælfric follows Augustine for the main outline of this sermon, and, as noted in the introductions to sermons II, III, and V, Pope views these and VI as belonging to a series of five Lenten sermons probably written before *Lives of Saints* (998) was completed.[1]

Ælfric uses numerology (lines 343ff.) to suggest the mystical union between Christ and his followers:

> Then the Savior said to them, "A day has twelve hours, and whoever walks during the day, his foot does not stumble because he sees the light of the world." Christ is that true Day and that true Light of all the world, and the person who follows Jesus does not walk in darkness but has the light of life. Christ's twelve apostles are the twelve hours serving the Lord during the day.[2]

This Lenten sermon promises that the truly penitent will meet the merciful God every time, Ælfric's quintessential theme: "This truth is very important. No sin is so great that a person cannot make amends for it here in this life, if he or she does penance according to the degree of the sin, trusting in God."[3] The sermon concludes with a signature Ælfrician awareness of his audience's limits: "We don't dare lengthen this sermon, nor weary you anymore with it because some of you might start complaining in your minds."

---

[1] Pope, *Homilies* I.165-67, 305-308; I.226.
[2] Pope, *Homilies* I.327-28 (VI.343-54).
[3] Pope, *Homilies* I.322 (VI.213-14).

Sermon VI

For the Sixth Day in the Fourth Week of Lent
John 11.1-45

The holy Gospel you heard read aloud today tells us about Lazarus, who lay sick in bed in his village of Bethany. And he was, as you know, the brother of Martha and Mary, and that was the Mary who with great reverence anointed our Lord with precious ointment and wiped his feet with her hair. Because Lazarus was bedridden, his worried sisters sent for the Savior immediately, saying, "Dear Lord, the one whom you love is now sick." He answered them, "This sickness will not result in death but is for God's glory, that the Son of God may be glorified through him."

The Savior intimately loved Martha and her sister Mary and their brother Lazarus, and yet, when he learned Lazarus was sick, Jesus did not leave where he was for two days. And after that he said to his disciples, "Now let's go again to the land of the Jews." Then his disciples said, "But, beloved teacher, just a few days ago the Jews tried to stone you, and yet you now wish to go back there again?"

And Jesus answered them: "Is it not true that a day has twelve hours in it? And whoever walks during the day does not stumble because he sees the light of this world. But whoever walks at night stumbles because there is no light in him." And then he spoke again, "Lazarus our friend lies now, sleeping, but I am going to go there, so I can wake him up."

Then his disciples said, "Lord, if he sleeps, he'll heal." But the Savior spoke about the death of Lazarus, who then lay dead. But Jesus's disciples thought their Lord spoke about sleep. Then Christ told them plainly: "Lazarus is dead. And for your sake, I am glad I was not there, so you may believe. However, let's go to him."

And then Thomas, whose family name was Didimus, said to his companions, "Let us also go, so that we may die with him." Then the Savior left, and they went with him. And on the fourth day after Lazarus had been buried, the Savior and his disciples came to the village of Bethany, where Lazarus was buried. Bethany was fifteen furlongs or almost two miles from Jerusalem.

Then many Jews visited Martha and Mary and comforted them because of their brother's death. When Martha heard the Savior was coming, she went out to meet him, but Mary sat at home. As soon as Martha saw the

Savior, she said: "Lord, if you'd been here, my brother would not be dead. But I know that even now God will grant you whatever you ask him."

And the Savior said, "Your brother will arise." And Martha said to him, "I know he will rise up in the resurrection on the last day." The Savior answered her: "I am the resurrection and the life. Whoever believes in me, even though he should die, will however live. And every person who lives and believes in me will not die in eternity. Do you believe this, Martha?"

She answered, "Yes, Lord, I believe you are Christ, the Son of God who should come into this world for men." After she had said this, she left immediately to get her sister, saying quietly, "The teacher is here, and he calls you."

Mary got up at once and went to Christ. And until Mary came to him, the Savior stayed in the same spot where he and Martha had spoken. Then the Jews followed Mary because they saw her get up quickly and supposed she wanted to weep at the tomb. As soon as Mary saw the Savior, she fell at his feet and said, "Lord, if you had been here, my brother would not be dead."

When the Savior saw her bitter tears, and the Jews who came with her weeping, he groaned in spirit and was troubled. He asked, "Where have you laid Lazarus?" And they answered, "Lord, come see." And then the Savior wept. The Jews said, "Look how he loved him." Some of them said, "Why, couldn't this man who healed that blind man have also prevented this one from dying?"

The Savior, grieving again in spirit, came to the tomb, and said to the bystanders, "Take the stone off it." Martha said to Christ, "Dear Lord, he stinks. It has been four days since we buried him." The Savior said to her, "Now, didn't I tell you that if you believe, you will see the glory of God?" So they quickly removed the tomb's stone cover.

And the Savior looked up as he prayed: "Father, I thank you, because you have heard me. I know without a doubt that you always hear me, but I have spoken this for the sake of those here who stand beside me, that they may believe you sent me." When he had said this, then he called loudly, *Lazare, ueni foras*: "Lazarus, come out here."

And immediately he who was dead stepped out of the tomb, his hands and feet still wrapped in strips of linen, as was customary, and his head was wrapped up in the small towel in which he had been buried. Then the Savior said to those watching, "Release his bonds, and let him go." And after that Lazarus lived a long time and was healthier than he had been before, through the Savior's might. Then many Jews visiting Mary and her sister Martha and seeing how the Savior raised their brother believed in Christ because of this living sign.

Of all the miracles our Savior did, this great miracle—that he raised the putrified Lazarus to life—is thought to be the greatest. But if we consider who raised him, then we will find ourselves rejoicing more than wondering. The One who made man raised that dead man. Christ is the only Son of the almighty Father, through whom all things were created. And in fact what sort of miracle is it for one person to be resurrected through Christ, when every day many people are born into this world by his might? It takes much more power to create many people than it does to raise one who had already been born.

And yet God humbled himself both in creating people and in raising them again from death. God created all people, and raised some, though he could have easily raised all the dead through his divine power, if he had wanted to. But he is keeping that work for himself at the end of this world, as he said in a certain Gospel: The time will come when all the dead in tombs will clearly hear the Son of God's voice and leave their tombs—those who did good, to the resurrection of life, and those who did evil, to the resurrection of condemnation.

Our Savior also daily accomplishes in our souls a second resurrection, which is when the soul rises up out of the death of sins because the soul of the person who sins cannot live unless it is revived again through confession and unless it pleases its Lord through penance. Every person dreads dying, and yet few dread the death of the soul. In order to sustain the life of a body, which may not be long, men and women work overtime on sea and on land so they can escape from death; and yet they will certainly die one day, even though they may run from death for a time. But they do not want to work towards not sinning, so their souls could live eternally without labor.

And the body of such a person is brought after Doomsday to the same life of labor, quickened in soul after Doomsday, forever. Though you may dread it, death will come to you. So it is wiser for you to guard against dying in an evil manner, brought to an end in sins, and ever afterwards suffering eternally in soul and body, endlessly punished, unable to die.

We now want to explain the soul's death. There are three kinds, though these are unknown to you. For the person who thinks of evil and desires to do evil, death lives secretly in his or her soul. And then there is the person who plots evil and does evil and is clearly soul-dead through evil. Finally, anyone who habitually and shamelessly sins and spreads evil is buried in rotten sins and in these indecent acts stinks terribly.

Now the book of Christ tells us that Christ our Savior raised three people from death to life. And these three people signified the threefold death of the sinful soul, which sins in three ways: by evil consent or evil thought, by evil performance, and by evil habit. Our Lord raised the daughter of one synagogue ruler. She lay secretly dead in his house and had not yet been carried out into public view. And she signified the death of the soul that happens within, through evil thought, and is not revealed through evil acts.

Then our Lord raised one young man when he came to a certain city called Naim. And this young man was carried out publically, and his mother followed him, sad and weeping. But our Lord immediately comforted her and was kind to her and raised her son and gave him to his mother because God is merciful. This dead person signified the death of the soul that sins openly, as if it carried its dead on a bier in the sight of other people, and then its sinful death is known through such unconcealed sins. If you sin, you must genuinely repent of it, and Christ will raise you so that you are alive in God, and he will give you to your mother, that is, to his church, in which you are baptized, and in which you will thrive.

The third dead person was the one whom our Lord raised, Lazarus the Jew. At that time he lay buried, stinking terribly, as we said earlier in this sermon. And he signified the sinful person who is in the habit of doing evil deeds, and stinks through bad reputation and evil habits. There are too many of these people who lie in sins, lost in bad habits and overwhelmed with wickedness, and they don't want to hear God's holy teaching. And the thought of trying to get out of the reeking dung seems tiresome to this sinful person, who much prefers to lie in the lusts of his or her body rather than to work towards giving up the lifestyle of unholy ease. As almighty God, our dear Savior can raise the souls of people who sin in these three ways, in the same manner that he raised the three dead persons to life through his divine might, bringing glory to himself.

This truth is very important. No sin is so great that a person cannot make amends for it here in this life, if he or she does penance according to the degree of the sin, trusting in God. But our Savior said in his Gospel that the person who speaks a blasphemous word against the Holy Spirit and holds God's Spirit to scorn never experiences God's forgiveness, neither in this world, nor in the one to come. Often heretics spoke foolishly about Christ, but later they made amends for it and submitted to him in true faith.

And he gave them forgiveness, as he said: "Though someone utters reproach or scorn concerning me, he is forgiven for such, if he repents of it. But whoever utters scorn or reproach about the Holy Spirit, then his sin never ends."

The almighty Father, who created all things, has one Son born ineffably from him alone, the true Savior. And the Holy Spirit is not called Son because he is one Father always without beginning, and his only begotten Son is of himself always, and the Holy Spirit is Will and Love of them both, ever with them and equally of them both. Now the Father is not Father of them both because one of them is his Son, and the other is not his Son. Again, the same Son is not Son of them both, that is, of the Father and of the Spirit, in the godhead. But the Holy Spirit alone is common to both of them, to the almighty Father and to his only begotten Son, and through that Spirit all sins are forgiven.

The wise Father created the world, and through his holy Wisdom, God's Son, he made all things. He also quickened them with life through the Holy Spirit, who is the Love of them both. Their works are ever indivisible, and they possess one godhead and one nature and one majesty. But the forgiveness of sins belongs to the Holy Spirit, who gives forgiveness to penitent persons and illuminates their minds with his gentle forgiveness and afterwards comforts them, because he is the Spirit of Comfort.

So the nativity belongs to Christ alone, as the forgiveness belongs to the living Spirit, who is almighty God ever without beginning, of the Father and of the Son, Love of them both. Concerning the Holy Spirit, you may all know that he is the all-ruling God, because he is so powerful that he can forgive the sins of all people who genuinely repent of their mistakes, throughout all the earth.

Only Christ the Savior assumed the nature of humanity and suffered for us so that now we can experience deliverance through that dear Lord and our forgiveness of sins through the Holy Spirit. And yet, we know for certain that the whole Trinity in true oneness accomplishes each of these works for us because they always all work one work.

The person who never ceases to act sinfully and who continues in his or her evil ways until the end of this life, despising the true Spirit's forgiveness, is speaking blasphemy and slander against the Holy Spirit. And the hardheartedness of this person's hostile mind bars the living way to the mercy of the merciful Spirit, and prevents that person from experiencing God's mercy. The Holy Spirit has mercy on all penitent persons, but he never has mercy on those who despise his grace.

Now with humble minds we must ask the almighty Father—who created us through his Wisdom and redeemed us through that same Son—to blot out our sins through the Holy Spirit and to protect us from Satan so we may grow in the God who made us. The deceitful devil, who schemes against humanity, sends evil, perverse thoughts against God into a person's heart because the devil wants to make everyone feel hopeless. Satan wants wicked thoughts to steal that person's faith in God's mercy. But everyone should realize evil thoughts cannot injure us if they do not please us and if we reject them and call out to our Lord.

A sinful person should never lose hope because of the magnitude of his or her sins. Nor should the good person presume too much on account of his or her goodness, exalting foolishly in the self. Nor should a good person despise a sinful person, because often the sinful person repents of evil deeds and the Lord raises that person up, as he did Lazarus. And then the penitent person lives a life better than those who had censured his sinful life earlier.

Concerning such, we read in one Gospel that there was a sinful woman who was very immoral, and when she discovered our Lord was with a certain Pharisee called Simon, she went there and drew near to Christ; and she lay at his feet and wept without ceasing. She washed his feet with her tears, and she wiped them with her hair, trembling. And then she anointed them with precious ointment, as was customary among the Jewish people. Then the Savior said that her many sins were forgiven because she loved much. But the person who loses faith and sins endlessly and dies hardhearted is without a doubt dead by the worst death because this person's endless sins result in his or her leaving this hard life only to enter eternal death.

We read about the three dead persons whom our Lord raised, but we remember that all of Jesus's miracles were not written down. However, one man did write down those miracles sufficient for the salvation of people and for their faith, as well as those that had exalted meaning, which were disclosed afterwards by the Savior. The Lord's apostles and their successors raised many people from death, but these miracles were done by that same Savior through them, as he had previously done by himself during his time as a man on this earth.

The sisters told Christ that Lazarus was sick and bedridden, but Christ stayed where he was and waited there a while until Lazarus was dead. Only afterwards did Christ go to him. He did not want to heal Lazarus but to raise him and through that great miracle manifest his powers. The disciples wanted to keep their Savior from going into danger because the Jews wanted to take him by ambush. And yet, in order to resurrect Lazarus, Jesus made the journey to Bethany. The holy apostles wanted to convince the Savior that he did not need to die, but Christ came voluntarily, intending to die so that the disciples and we also would not need to die an evil death. Christ delivered us from all that.

Then the Savior said to them, "A day has twelve hours, and whoever walks during the day, his foot does not stumble because he sees the light of the world." Christ is that true Day and that true Light of all the world, and the person who follows Jesus does not walk in darkness but has the light of life. Christ's twelve apostles are the twelve hours serving the Lord during the day, even though the deceitful Judas, who afterwards betrayed him, fell down from that honor; however, another person took his place—Matthias the Humble. And the twelvefold number was again completed in the twelve apostles.

The Savior said to Martha, Lazarus's sister: "I am the resurrection and the life. Whoever believes in me, even though he should die, will still live. And every person who lives and believes in me will not die in eternity." And Jesus said in another place, *Ego sum Deus Abraham et Deus Isáác et Deus Iacob*: "I am the God of Abraham and of Isaac and of Jacob." Christ is not the God of dead men, but the God of the living. All people live in God's Son because anyone who believes in Christ, though that person should die, will live. And yet whoever does not believe in Jesus, though that person may be alive, he or she is still dead in that evil death.

We don't dare lengthen this sermon, nor weary you anymore with it because some of you might start complaining in your minds. But let us all pray to Christ our Lord that he raise our souls from sins and give us eternal life at the end.

To him be glory and praise forever. Amen.

Introduction to Sermon VII

Sermon VII exegetes John 16:5-14, Christ's last instructions to his disciples before his Crucifixion. Sermons VII, VIII, IX, X, and XII (for consecutive Sundays from the fourth Sunday after Easter to the first Sunday after Pentecost) were probably finished by Ælfric towards the middle of his monkhood, sometime after *Lives of Saints* (998) and shortly before he became abbot of Eynsham in 1005.[1] Sermon VII could well have been written just before the first millennium, then, a possibility that would have made its valedictory tone and promise of comfort from the Holy Spirit especially significant, even urgent for both Ælfric and audience.

A most poignant passage starts at line 127, very likely an independent development by Ælfric drawn perhaps from his general knowledge of the Scripture and scriptural exegesis;[2] it shows Ælfric's concern to make the humanity of God's Son real:

> And the risen Christ lived with them forty days. During this time, they felt him, holding his hands and feet with their hands, to see he was indeed made of solid stuff. They inspected the scars on his side, too. And they saw Christ had risen up in a perfect body, vanquishing death. They saw he had every limb, and he still does, absolutely. Christ stood on his feet, and they were not without legs. They felt Christ's sides, and he really had both belly and chest, without which no sides may be seen. Christ also had a belly, since he ate and drank, and he had a tongue, since he spoke to them. And he was not without teeth, which help the tongue make sounds, and Jesus had a throat, since others heard his voice. And they held his hands and noticed Christ's arms and shoulders on his solid, perfect body. There could be no deficiency in any of the limbs of the benevolent Savior after his resurrection, since he promised us all that after we die an earthly death and rise up out of death on Doomsday, we will not lose then even the littlest hair from our body that we had on earth.[3]

This detailed description of Christ's earthly body is an Anglo-Saxon forerunner of later medieval mystic obsessions, as evident in St. Birgitta of Sweden's *Prayers*:

> Joy and eternal praise be to you, Lord Jesus Christ. Your gorgeous forehead never turned away from what was right and true. Blessed be your forehead! May all creatures praise it. Amen. Your bright, compassionate eyes look kindly on all who ask you for grace and mercy, in love. Blessed be your eyes, eyelids, and wonderful eyebrows! May your lovely, kind vision be praised for-

---

[1] Pope, *Homilies* I.332.
[2] Pope, *Homilies* I.338-39.
[3] Pope, *Homilies* I.346-47 (VII.127-61).

ever. Amen. Your sympathetic ears are happy to listen to everyone who speaks humbly. Blessed be your ears. May they always be filled with good words. Amen. Your very clean teeth chewed physical food sensibly for the nourishing of your holy body. May your teeth be blessed and honored by every creature. Amen. You never used your tongue poorly, and you never kept quiet except honestly and helpfully. You always said whatever God wanted you to say. Blessed be your tongue. Amen. My Lord Jesus Christ, blessed be your throat, stomach, and intestines. May all your sacred internal workings be honored because they fed you well and kept your precious body functioning efficiently. They nourished your bodily life for the redemption of souls, and to the angels' joy. Amen. You, Lord, are our leader because on your sacred shoulders and neck you carried the weight of the Cross before you smashed the gates of hell forever. Blessed be your neck and shoulders for enduring so much. Amen.[4]

† † †

---

[4]Carmen Acevedo Butcher, *Incandescence: 365 Readings with Women Mystics* (Orleans MA: Paraclete Press, 2005) April 12.

Sermon VII

For the Fourth Sunday after Easter
John 16.5-14

Mass often celebrates one of the many Gospel texts from the long speech our dear Savior spoke on the night he was betrayed, as written down by John, who witnessed it all. Today we will discuss one of these Gospel texts. We want to tell you the Savior's own words of advice, as he himself spoke them. Christ said to his followers on that night of betrayal: "I am now going to the One who sent me here, but none of you asks me where I am going now, though your hearts are sorrowful because I have said this to you. I tell you the truth—it benefits you that I go away like this."

And he also told them: "If I do not leave you, the Spirit of Comfort will not come to you. If I go away, I will be sure to send him to you. When he comes, as soon as he comes, God's Spirit will convict this world of its guilt regarding sin, righteousness, and true judgment. God's Spirit will show the world its guilt concerning sin because they do not believe in me. He will show the world its guilt concerning righteousness because I am now going up to my Father, and you won't see me anymore. He will show the world its guilt concerning judgment because the evil prince of this world is now judged.

"I have so many more things to tell you, but you cannot understand them, nor bear them in your hearts now. However, when the Spirit of truth comes, he will teach you all truth. He will not speak of himself. He will speak whatever he hears, and he will be sure to make known to you the things that are to come. He certainly glorifies me because he will receive from me the things that he will tell you."

We will now explain this scriptural lesson more clearly. The Savior said he would be going to his heavenly Father who sent him. And his companions had no need to wonder about that because all of them clearly saw him ascending effortlessly up into heaven, the cloud received him with ease, and they were looking on and saw all this and knew it was no illusion.

"Your hearts are sad because I have told you this." The disciples grieved to let their dear Savior go. And it would have been especially difficult for them to do without his nearness because at that time they were not yet comforted by the Holy Spirit, as they were afterwards.

"I tell you the truth—it benefits you that I go away in this manner." And Jesus also said to them: "If I do not go away from you, the Spirit of Comfort will not come to you. It benefits you much that I remove my human form from your sight, so that later through faith you can have more love for me. Then your hearts will desire the heavenly home, to which I myself first make a journey now. If I do not leave you, the Spirit of Comfort will not come to you."

While living with them on earth, Jesus could very easily have given them that same Spirit of Comfort, as he did later when he had arisen out of death. Christ then breathed on them all and said: "Now receive in you that holy Spirit of Comfort. And the people to whom you give forgiveness of sins, their sins are forgiven immediately. Those to whom you do not give forgiveness of sins, they are not forgiven." He gave all his apostles this authority.

But they would not have possessed a great desire for heavenly life had the Savior not first ascended up to heaven with them watching. And afterwards, out of heaven Jesus sent them that Holy Spirit, as he had promised them. The Holy Spirit lived in the holy prophets who prophesied about Christ according to the former law, and God's Spirit also lived in Christ's apostles intimately. But the Holy Spirit was most revealed to these first ministers of God who proclaimed the Gospel to humanity. To the disciples, God's Spirit appeared as a shining brightness, like a burning fire.

"When he comes, as soon as he comes, God's Spirit will convict this world of its guilt regarding sin, righteousness, and true judgment." While living among people on earth, the Savior did reveal all these things to those who heard his word; however, at that time he himself only convicted the Jewish people, to whom he was come. Christ lived with them and worked many miracles among them. After the Holy Spirit had been sent to Jesus's holy apostles and lived in them, without exception God's Spirit convicted all the world in regard to these three things the Savior spoke of.

"He will convict the world of its guilt concerning sin because they do not believe in me." Unbelief—when someone does not believe in the living Savior—is the origin of sins. And belief is the beginning of all good virtues because belief leads us to heaven. For those people who saw Christ's miracles, it was a great sin if they did not wish to believe in the dear Savior, who raised dead persons through his divine power and worked many other miracles for them.

The prophet and the psalmist of old sang about these things even before the Savior had become a man here in this world. They spoke of the Jews and their presumption, saying: *Sagitte paruulorum facte sunt plage eorum.* The prophet said that their deeds and the wounds the Jews maliciously gave the Savior were similar to those given by children who in their callow playing shoot with reeds on the playground.

Who is so foolish or so weak-witted to think the true Judge could be condemned or the God who unbinds all humanity could be bound? And who would want to kill the One who forgives our sins and who raised the dead through his divine power? And later on Doomsday we will all be raised through Christ. The Jews' schemes against the Savior were foolish because they decided they would try to kill the One who with his holy resurrection overpowered death, for our deliverance.

Et infirmate sunt contra eos lingue eorum: "And their tongues were robbed of health, to the detriment of themselves." The prophet said this. Their tongues were very sick because they said this about the true Savior: "If he is the Son of God, he should come off the cross." And afterwards the watchmen stationed around Christ's tomb declared God's Son rose up alive from the tomb. Their faithlessness made them ask for a lesser thing. They wanted Christ to come down off the cross, and live, but afterwards he obviously rose up out of death, and this was a great miracle. God's Son won certain victory from the old devil. And Jesus saved us from eternal death and from the power of the devil.

We also want to tell you something else you should know. After Christ's own death and after his rising up out of death, our dear Savior lived here in this world with his holy apostles, and in many ways the risen Christ taught them how they must teach all humanity to have faith. Christ taught them how to teach the world right belief—how to bow towards baptism and away from their former sins, so that the world could have eternal life with Christ, as he promised all who love him. After the resurrection, Jesus ate and drank openly with the disciples, and through his actions he showed them that he was in fact actually alive after his own death, which he had overpowered with divine might.

And the risen Christ lived with them forty days. During this time, they felt him, holding his hands and feet with their hands, to see he was indeed made of solid stuff. They inspected the scars on his side, too. And they saw Christ had risen up in a perfect body, vanquishing death. They saw he had every limb, and he still does, absolutely.

Christ stood on his feet, and they were not without legs. They felt Christ's sides, and he really had both belly and chest, without which no sides may be seen. Christ also had a belly, since he ate and drank, and he had a tongue, since he spoke to them. And he was not without teeth, which help the tongue make sounds, and Jesus had a throat, since they heard his voice. And they held his hands and noticed Christ's arms and shoulders on his solid, perfect body. There could be no deficiency in any of the limbs of the benevolent Savior after his resurrection, since he promised us all that after we die an earthly death and rise up out of death on Doomsday, we will not lose then even the littlest hair from our body that we had on earth.

"God's Spirit will show the world its guilt concerning righteousness because I am now going up to my Father, and you will not see me anymore." True righteousness is when a person rightly believes in the true Savior, the One his followers saw and believed and honored with love. We have not seen him, but still, with faith, we believe in the true Creator who created us as humans and afterwards delivered us from the devil's power. And this is righteousness for us.

"God's Spirit will show the world its guilt concerning judgment because the evil prince of this world is now judged." The hawkish devil is referred to as the "prince of the world" because Satan has much sovereignty over the unrighteous who love this world more than they love the Creator who created it. In spite of this fact, the devil in no way has all of this world in his power, but almighty God possesses the entire sphere of the earth and those who live on it and those who always bring honor to him with good works.

Satan was condemned through the passion of our Lord because Jesus took Adam's offspring away from him and gave his apostles power over him, so that they could drive out the devil from those who were mad and trample on the devil's power. And Satan could not harm them anywhere.

"I have so many more things to tell you, but you cannot understand them, nor bear them in your hearts." After his resurrection, Jesus said many things to his apostles that they could not have easily understood before they had actually seen the Savior with them whole after death, eating and drinking and speaking his teaching to them in clear words.

"When the Spirit of Truth comes, he will teach you all truth." Through the Holy Spirit, the holy apostles became so learned they spoke with all the languages of unknown peoples. And with much meaning of spiritual significance, as God revealed to them, they were able to teach humanity in the world from the old books they had not known earlier under Moses's law. It is true that no person on earth can manage in this life to understand all truth until he or she has come to the true God, as Paul, the teacher of the Gentiles, said to us.

"He will not speak of himself, but will speak whatever he hears." As the Savior said, the Holy Spirit does not speak separate from those with whom he exists in one godhead. The Spirit is the great Love and the mighty Will of the Father and of the Son, of them both equally. And all of the prophets prophesied through him, and the holy apostles spoke through him, greatly stirred and made bold by God's Spirit.

"And he will make known to you the things that are to come." As we said before, prophecy is from the Holy Spirit. And he revealed to the prophets and to the apostles the things that were to come. And God's Spirit illuminated their minds with his great grace.

"He glorifies me because he receives from me the things he will tell you." The Holy Spirit glorified Christ's humanity because his grace is found in God's holy home, and God's love is poured out in our hearts through that same Spirit, who is the Love of God, of the Father and of the Son, common to them always, in one majesty, forever. Amen.

Introduction to Sermon VIII

Ælfric finished sermon VIII sometime during the middle of his monastic career, between the completion of *Lives of Saints* (998) and his becoming abbot of Eynsham in 1005.[1] His pedagogical predilection for definition shows in his treatment of *godspell* in lines 3-7;[2] and in a passage beginning at line 73, he makes what Pope calls "a substantial addition to the exegesis of the gospel" by going beyond his source material in Bede and Haymo to compose a bold passage on prayer, an important addition to this sermon for the fifth Sunday after Easter, followed as it is by the three Rogation Days:

> How did the excellent apostles get great things from the holy Father? They asked. And here is what they received after the Savior's ascension: The disciples raised the dead in the name of their Lord, as he himself had done while on earth. And they worked various miracles in his name, and they converted the Gentiles to faith in Christ. And also the prophet Elijah once asked almighty God to withhold rain showers for three-and-a-half years because of the people's cruelty. And later, when the people had turned their hearts to God with greater faith, Elijah asked God to send them rain showers and earthly fruits.[3]

---

[1] Pope, *Homilies* I.332. See the introductions to VII, IX, X, and XII.
[2] Pope, *Homilies* I.357 (VIII.3-7).
[3] Pope, *Homilies* I.353 (VIII.73ff.).

Sermon VIII

For the Fifth Sunday after Easter
John 16.23-30

Because of their ignorance, some people do not know for certain why the Gospel is called that. They don't know what *Gospel* means. "Gospel" is God's own teaching and the words Christ spoke in this world to humanity for teaching and right belief. And because God came to earth, the Gospel is literally a very "good story." That's why it makes us very happy to hear the Gospel describe how we will be allowed to enjoy the heavenly home with God always, as he promised everyone who loves him by seeking him honestly, trusting in his truth.

Today we should listen to the holy Gospel text with penitent hearts, for our improvement. We should also learn what the words mean, so we can more easily convert them into good works. A wise person's good deeds reveal God's holy law and teaching, while the unrighteous person hears the words but never wants to convert them into the necessary good works.

On Thursday evening before Easter, our Savior had a very long talk with his disciples before he suffered, and at his departure he told them many truths. And John the Evangelist, who heard our Savior's teaching, set them all down in the book of Christ. At that time Jesus spoke these words to his disciples: *Euuangelium; Amen, amen, dico uobis; si quid petieritis Patrem in nomine meo, dabit uobis. Et reliqua*: "I tell you the truth, if you ask for anything for yourselves from my holy Father in my name, he will surely give it to you immediately. You have not yet asked for anything in my name. Ask and you will receive, that your joy may be full. I have spoken to you in parables. But the time will come when I will not speak to you in parables. I will clearly make known to you concerning the true Father. On that day you will earnestly ask in my name. And I have not yet told you that I petition that same Father on your behalf, interceding for you. The Father loves you because you loved me and you believed I have come from God. I came out from the Father and am come to earth. I am leaving this world now, and I am going to the Father."

Then his followers's joy increased, and they said: "Now you speak clearly, dear friend. You are not speaking to us in parables today. Now we know for sure you know all things and there is no need for you to be asked anything. That's why we believe you came from God."

We have briefly recounted this holy Gospel in English, as you have just heard it. We have told you only the naked words. Now we want to adorn them for you with beautiful meaning, so their teaching will please you, if you receive their spiritual sense with good will.

"I tell you the truth, if you ask for anything for yourselves from my holy Father in my name, he will surely give it to you immediately." From his childhood, the Savior was called "Jesus" by the holy angel, before he was even born. And the person who asks Jesus for salvation is asking "in his name" because *Jesus* means "Savior." Pray in the Savior's name now for salvation of mind and body, or pray for a dear friend, and the Father will certainly grant you the desire of your heart, if you and your prayers do not displease him.

If you are evil, you must stop doing evil and submit to the good Father with goodness. And if you pray for something evil for another person, you are not praying as the Savior commanded. Instead, with an evil heart you are desiring evil. That is not salvation in the Savior's name.

How did the excellent apostles get great things from the holy Father? They asked. And here is what they received after the Savior's ascension: The disciples raised the dead in the name of their Lord, as he himself had done while on earth. And they worked various miracles in his name, and they converted the Gentiles to faith in Christ. And also the prophet Elijah once asked almighty God to withhold rain showers for three-and-a-half years because of the people's cruelty. And later, when the people had turned their hearts to God with greater faith, Elijah asked God to send them rain showers and earthly fruits.

In another Gospel, the beloved Savior described for his holy apostles the great petitions people can receive by asking God for them. Such requests please God. The Savior said: *Amen, dico uobis, quia si quis dixerit huic monti, Tollere et mittere in máre et non hesitauerit in corde suo, sed crediderit, quia quodcumque dixerit fiat fiet ei*: "I tell you the truth, if anyone speaking earnestly tells a particular mountain in my name: 'In the name of God go far out into the sea,' and if this person does not doubt that what he has asked for will be granted, but if he believes in his heart, then whatever he asks for will come to pass." Though this is an amazing, miraculous request for a mountain to remove itself from where it is, and by the power of a mere person, we can tell you it certainly did happen once through one holy man, as we will now tell you.

There was a certain holy bishop named Gregory, an esteemed teacher, highly honored. I spoke of him once in another sermon, how he approached a heathen god—who had no divinity—and drove him away from his idol. This same Gregory wanted to build a holy monastery for God near a certain river, and the spot he chose was quite suitable for the monastery, except for a very high cliff near where he wanted to build. There was not enough room for that work of God.

So the bishop marked out on the mountain the portion of land he wanted to have as the extent of that work. And then he asked the Almighty, who can do what he wants, to lift up the mountain according to his marking, so that Gregory could build his monastery on that cleared space. And God immediately removed the mountain without difficulty, as Gregory wished. And the holy man built a monastery for God there.

There were also two brothers, well-to-do in life, and in a large lake they had a fishery common to them both for greater profit. But at the pool, arguments and murders and great fights often occurred because of the fishery. This bloodshed made the bishop most unhappy, so he asked God to change the water into pleasant arable land. And immediately the water left the fishery, and the lake became large fields. Then a person could plow what was once the fishery, and ever afterwards grain grew there in peace.

Julian the Apostate, who was first a Christian and was tonsured as a priest because of the fear of Caesar, rejected his faith and believed in pagan gods after he was his own master. And he became Caesar and loved sorcery and serving the devil, and he killed many martyrs and fought against the Savior until he died. One day Julian the Apostate sent a devil to a certain country on some errand, and he told the devil to hurry. And this devil carried out his mission and in ten days returned to Julian the Apostate.

Then Caesar asked this devil, "Why are you so late?" The devil answered: "I was hindered from doing evil by a holy monk called Publius. I couldn't finish your errand because that monk blocked my way with his many prayers. And so I had to turn back, returning to you in ignorance, with no message." Then Caesar was killed on the way there. And when some of his thanes heard this news, they went to that monk Publius and became monks themselves. Mighty prayers bring about such things through the true God, who is always kind to us and hears the prayers of his saints in need. And God is never unfriendly. He never rejects a beggar's cries.

The Gospel text also tells us that the Savior said, "You have not yet asked for anything in my name." They had not yet asked for anything in the Savior's name because at that time they had Christ with them, and they were enjoying his teaching. That's why the disciples didn't yet feverishly ask for unseen things: They still had him in their sights.

"Ask and you will receive, that your joy may be full." Christ then commanded them to ask for eternal joy because no person ever experiences perfect happiness during this life, since something always ails us here.

"I have spoken to you in parables. But the time will come when I will not speak to you in parables, but I will clearly make known to you the true Father." Books will often tell a parable, which is one thing in words, and another thing in meaning. And the Savior spoke to his disciples in many parables because he wanted to strengthen their hearts. But then Christ did tell them he clearly wanted to make the holy Father known to them, because when God's saints live with him, Christ allows them to see his Father and his glory, as the angels see him now.

"On that day you will earnestly ask in my name." A person's life is like a day that never ends. And anyone who petitions God during this life on earth is asking in the daytime, not in the black darkness of temptations. The person who petitions God here on earth understands the words the Savior also spoke to his disciples in one of his Gospels, *Ego et Pater unum sumus*: "I and my Father are truly one." They are in fact one God, in one godhead. And always common to them both is one true Love, the Holy Spirit, who goes out from them both.

Christ said, "We are," because the Son is always living and does not change from the Father and the Spirit, nor is any one of the three changed to another, so that he is different from that which he was before. Jesus said, "We are one," because of the oneness, because the one godhead and the one majesty and the one nature common to them all is not willing to permit they are three gods but one Almighty God always in three persons.

And the saints will know this is true when they see him. It was not the holy Father who was born as man for us, nor did the Father suffer for us, but the Son suffered, he who alone assumed our humanity. And here we are able to learn that they are three, and yet one God, as we read aloud earlier.

The Gospel text also records these words of the Savior, "And I have not yet told you that I petition that same Father on your behalf, interceding for you." In the humanity with which Jesus was invested, he pleads with his heavenly Father on behalf of God's saints, and in Christ's divinity, where he is God, he always grants all things with the Father. And in the Son we have a very good intercessor.

"That very same Father loves you because you loved me and believed I have come from God." Here you may learn that the person who does not have the Son does not have the Father who sent him, and the Father loves those who believe in Christ. And anyone who accepts such love is happy.

"I came out from the Father and am come to earth. I am leaving this world now, and I am going to the Father." He came to earth and was visibly man, he who was unseen with the true Father. And Christ left this world, when in his human form he ascended up to the unseen. But until the end of this world, Christ still lives with his holy people through his divine nature, as he himself promised. And Christ never deceives. If you question how he can live simultaneously with people on earth and also in heaven, then look at the sun, God's creation, and see how it is able to send its shining rays from its heavenly orbit all over this earth. A sunbeam shines down clearly on each one of you, and if you love the Omnipotent God, can't he send you his light, and love you like this?

When the joy of our Savior's followers grew, they said: "Now you are speaking clearly, dear friend, not in parables today." Now that you have heard what they said, how can we explain this truth to you any more clearly than the apostles said it?

"Now we know you know all truths and there is no need for you to be asked anything." They spoke sincerely about the true Savior. They knew that as Omnipotent God Christ knew all things. And this is the manifestation of his true godhead. Christ can scrutinize the hearts of all people and see all our thoughts. And we do not need to ask how he himself wishes to act.

Then the apostles said, and so should we, "Because of these things, we believe you came from God." And we must believe in the living Savior, so the Father who sent him may love us and illuminate our hearts with the grace of the Holy Spirit, to whom is ever one glory and one honor. Amen.

Introduction to Sermon IX

Sermon IX was completed during the middle of Ælfric's monkhood, after *Lives of Saints* (998) and before the start of his Eynsham abbacy in 1005.[1] At line 48 of this sermon for the Sunday after the ascension of the Lord, Ælfric cogently articulates Anglo-Saxon kingship ideals:

> [T]he king is Christ's true vicar over the Christian people who Christ himself redeemed. The king is himself hallowed as their shepherd. With his people's help, the king ought to protect them against an attacking army and ask the true Savior for victory for them, as all kings have done who pleased God. The Savior has given the king such authority under himself. Every king is holy who protects God's people and governs with love, not cruelty, but always according to what is right, not by self-will. And, if the need is great, the king is always willing to give his own life as a last measure to protect his people, as the Savior gave himself for us, though he could have saved all humanity without his own death and could have taken his creation away from the devil, if Christ had wanted to.[2]

Writing this passage, Ælfric probably reflected wistfully on the peaceful Viking-free years of King Edgar's godly reign (AD 959–975), when the Benedictine Reform and learning flourished.

Ælfric's love of numerology and classification as pedagogical tools are also seen here at lines 121-49 in the listing of the seven traditionally patristic gifts of the Spirit, a recurring theme for this monk.[3]

† † †

---

[1] Pope, *Homilies* I.332. See the introductions to sermons VII, VIII, X, and XII.
[2] Pope, *Homilies* I.380-81 (IX.48ff).
[3] Pope, *Homilies* I.384-85 (IX.121-49); see also I.297 (V.208-13); I.418 (XI.68); and II.121-23 (XVII.572).

Sermon IX

For the Sunday after the Ascension of the Lord
John 15.26-16

While the Savior was here in this world, he lived among his holy apostles and other people and worked many miracles, and on the very night before the morning on which he suffered, Christ spoke these words to his followers at his departure: "When the Spirit of Comfort comes whom I will send to you from my Father—he is the Spirit of truth and genuinely proceeds from the true Father—this Spirit will very clearly give testimony concerning me, that is, that he is witness of all my good works. And you also bear witness of me, because you have lived with me from the beginning. I have spoken these things to you so you will not be made to stumble. They will banish you from their synagogues, for the time will come when those who kill you will believe that in doing so they are serving God. And they will do these things because of their ignorance, because they do not know my Father or me. But I have spoken these things to you so when their time comes, you may be mindful that I told you of them."

The Savior always spoke openly to his companions and often to the people of his nation, teaching them skillfully. He wanted people to know what things they should guard against. He also wanted to show those people who wish to fulfill their Lord's words with works how they can do the will of their Lord.

You can hear what he himself said about these things, *Ego palam locutus sum mundo. Et reliqua*: "I have spoken openly to this world. I have always taught in the synagogue and in the temple, where the Jews all came together, and I have not said anything in secret."

Also, Christ genuinely taught them by example. He taught them that prophets and those who advise many people must declare their words of advice openly, not through secret whisperings, because many people together are able to make better decisions than individuals can through their own will. The wisdom of God in books also commands us, *Omnia cum consilio fac, et post factum non paenitebis*: "Decide all issues properly through consultation, and after the deed, nothing at all will cause you regret."

The wise person who knows good counsel must never hide his or her wisdom: *Sapientia abscondita et thesaurus occultus, quae utilitas in utroque?*—"How can either hidden wisdom or concealed treasure help anyone?" And the king must call on his wise councillors. And he should act according to their advice, not following secret whisperings, because the king is Christ's true vicar over the Christian people who Christ himself redeemed. The king is himself hallowed as their shepherd. With his people's help, the king ought to protect them against an attacking army and ask the true Savior for victory for them, as all kings have done who pleased God. The Savior has given the king such authority under himself.

Every king is holy who protects God's people and governs with love, not cruelty, but always according to what is right, not by self-will. And, if the need is great, the king is always willing to give his own life as a last measure to protect his people, as the Savior gave himself for us, though he could have saved all humanity without his own death and could have taken his creation away from the devil, if Christ had wanted to.

The Savior once asked his holy apostles who did men of the world say he was. They answered, "Some say you are John the Baptist, some Elijah, some Jeremiah or a certain prophet." Then the Savior asked, "Who do you say I am?" With a steady heart Peter answered him, "You are the true Christ, the living Son of God."

We have explained these words in another sermon with clear sense, but now we will again discuss them here. The Savior has shown us by example that we ought to know what sort of name or reputation we possess because of the way we live. And we should always incline ourselves to the more excellent ways of behaving. We do not want to become evil examples to others by being cruel or having too strong a will, because an evil example is obviously damaging. Again the Savior said, "I have given you an example—as I have treated you, you yourselves should treat others."

The Savior also said, as this Gospel says to us, "When the Spirit of Comfort comes whom I will send to you from my Father—who is the Spirit of truth and intimately proceeds from the true Father; God's Spirit will very clearly give testimony concerning me, that is, that he is witness of all my works." Before the Savior came to earth in his human form, the true nature of the holy Trinity was not clearly understood, but Christ often told others about his heavenly Father and about the Holy Spirit, thus revealing their true nature. And Christ himself spoke with others about this, clearly explaining it to them, as you have heard here in this Gospel text.

In another place, as Matthew wrote down, Christ told his holy apostles, instructing them with these words, *Euntes ergo docete omnes gentes, baptizantes eos in nomine Patris, et Filii, et Spiritus sancti; et reliqua*: "Go out to distant lands. Teach all nations, and baptize faithfully in the name of the Father, and of his Son, and of the Holy Spirit." The Son of God said this. These words of the Savior himself are an excellent explanation of true belief. Christ commanded all peoples to be baptized in the holy Trinity and in true oneness. And this is one belief for all people to keep faithfully, that is, for those who possess any love for God.

Christ said he wanted to send to us the Spirit of Truth who proceeds from the Father because the Spirit of Comfort proceeds from both Father and Son and is Love of them both and is just as powerful as they both are. The Son sent the Spirit and said he would certainly bear witness of Christ. Both Father and Son sent the Spirit, and he came voluntarily because this same Spirit is the one who—as Almighty Ruler, and by means of his divinity—distributes his spiritual gifts all over this world among God's people, mightily. And the Spirit sows his seven gifts among us, in ways that please him. And we prepare ourselves for his indwelling by cultivating kindness within ourselves and a temperament bent on serving others.

The Savior left much to the testimony of the Holy Spirit, that is, to his witness, because while Christ was in human form on this earth, he often honored both the heavenly Father and the Holy Spirit, as John's Gospel chiefly tells us, in the fourth book of Christ, written down by John himself. The Holy Spirit gave witness to Christ first to the apostles in the upper room, when in the likeness of fire the Spirit enveloped them all and kindled their passions. As a person can make iron glow—but not be consumed—by intense heat, so did the disciples burn with inward love. By God's grace then, the disciples were miraculously informed about the humanity of Christ, and they boldly proclaimed to kings and noblemen about the events of the Savior's life. And his Spirit always strengthened them in all truth.

God's gifts are amazing in seven ways: in wisdom; in understanding; in good counsel; in the resoluteness of a strong heart; in true knowledge; in good behavior; and in divine respect and submission. We spoke more clearly about these gifts long ago. God gladdens our minds with good intention, and through him we recognize what we need to do. And God also strengthens us for the performance of good deeds, so no difficulty will stop our doing good to others. And the person who does not have Christ's Spirit does not belong to Christ.

"And you also bear witness of me because you have lived with me from the beginning." The Holy Spirit in them made them bold. And their having lived with the Lord of glory during his life on earth, from the beginning of his teaching, also strengthened their singleness of mind. Without a doubt they could declare to humanity what they had heard and had seen themselves.

Peter referred to these events in his preaching. He said on one occasion, "Out of death Christ rose up on the third day, and he was manifested to us, not to all people, but to us who ate and drank with him after he arose from death whole." Christ wanted to have as witnesses for himself both the holy prophets who prophesied about him in the former dispensation—before he had come to all people on earth—and also afterwards his apostles, as we told you here. And the holy martyrs are Christ's witnesses. They gave their lives and were killed because of faith in him. And every honest teacher is Christ's witness for truth against any false heretics who loved error or who still love it.

"I have spoken these things to you so you will not be made to stumble. They will banish you from their synagogues." A person is made to stumble who—influenced by evil examples—falls into despair, robbed of hope, and is then captured by sinful deeds. Everyone must be on guard against the influence of a bad example. Now the Savior warned his apostles about the coming temptation, when leaders of their synagogues would persecute them, outlawing and driving them completely out, as the Jews did later. They beat the apostles and banned their preaching anything about the Savior anywhere. But the disciples would not stop preaching. They said it was more fitting to obey the Lord than men. And so that's what they did.

"For the time will come when those who kill you will believe they are serving God." The Jews who had fought against the Savior believed they could fulfill the law of Moses by killing Christ's heralds, who proclaimed the Gospel under God's grace, in the new dispensation, which the Jews did not understand.

Then their cruelty led them to stone Stephen to death and also the righteous James. And they also beheaded the other James and persecuted the other apostles. And their sinful outbursts of hatred showed how the Jews rejected the apostles' teaching, and with a vengeance.

"And they will do these things because of their ignorance, because they do not know my Father or me." The Jews did not want to know our Lord with true faith. They chose not to understand he is the Son of God, and their too-strong wills made them contradict Christ's words. And now they do not accept either the Father or the Son, as Jesus said in another Gospel: "The person who hates me hates my Father. But I have spoken these things to you so when their time comes, you may remember I told you." The Savior warned them about the coming fight. He knew we can more easily withstand hardships that are foretold, than the unexpected troubles that come suddenly upon us.

And it was a great comfort to the apostles in the future fight that this warning had come from the very One who could always help them achieve victory in conflict and, afterwards, happiness and eternal honor in glory with him who reigns forever. Amen.

Introduction to Sermon X

Except for the very Ælfrician introduction of two riveting negative exempla at line 159, sermon X is a straightforward exposition of its pericope, John 14.23-31.[1] This sermon was completed sometime between 998 and 1005.[2]

At lines 59-61, Ælfric clearly presents the leitmotif of his entire prodigious corpus: "The love that loves God is not idle. Instead, it is strong and works great things always. And if love isn't willing to work, then it isn't love."[3] Ever the communicator, Ælfric also shows his preference for definition as a simple pedagogical aid when he discusses the Greek and Latin ecclesiastical terms, *Paraclete* and *Consolator*: "The Holy Spirit is called *Paraclete* in the Greek language, and in Latin *Consolator*, which means 'Comforter' in English. He is called these things because he comforts the hearts of those who repent of their sins (lines 83-86)."[4]

The negative exempla (at lines 159ff.) show Ælfric's penchant for telling the stories of heretics like Arrius and Olympius as examples for his congregation not to follow. Through these striking foils, he outlines the painful estrangement to be experienced—not by his good congregation, of course—but by anyone who disobeys God.[5]

Ælfric also uses these vivid stories to remind his congregation the foes of God struggle against the Almighty in vain. Certain destruction comes to those who want "to belittle the dear Savior."[6] God is, he stresses, always triumphant. Ælfric had already told the story of Arrius in *Catholic Homilies I*, and to do so had most likely consulted Haymo's *Historiæ Sacræ Epitome*, though this well-read Anglo-Saxon monk was also familiar with Haymo's chief sources, Rufinus and the *Historia Tripartita*, while Isidore's *Chronicon* presents all the details Ælfric needed for his exemplum on Olympius.[7]

To reinforce his theme of the victorious God, Ælfric briefly mentions the harrowing-of-hell topos in the penultimate paragraph of this Pentecost Sunday sermon.[8] For a fuller treatment of this topos, see the introduction to sermon IV and its text.[9]

---

[1] Pope, *Homilies* I.393.
[2] Pope, *Homilies* I.332. See introductions to VII, VIII, IX, and XII.
[3] Pope, *Homilies* I.398 (X.59-61).
[4] Pope, *Homilies* I.399-400 (X.83-86).
[5] Pope, *Homilies* I.403 (X.159ff.).
[6] Pope, *Homilies* I.403 (homily X.160).
[7] Pope, *Homilies* I.394-95.
[8] Pope, *Homilies* I.404 (X.197ff.).
[9] Pope, *Homilies* I.274-5 (IV.188-96); cf. I.348 (VII.181-86).

Sermon X

For Pentecost Sunday
John 14.23-31

John the Evangelist wrote down this Gospel, and in it he said on one occasion while the Savior was here in this world that Christ spoke these words to his apostles: "Whoever absolutely loves me will keep my words, and my Father will love him. And we will come to him, and we will both certainly live with him. Whoever does not love me will not keep my words. And the teaching you have heard is not my word but comes from the same Father who sent me. I have spoken these things to you while I am still living with you. The holy Spirit of Comfort whom my Father will send to you in my name is the One who will teach you all things. God's Spirit will make everything that I said to you clear. I leave you peace. I give you my peace. I do not give you the world's peace. So don't let your hearts worry. Don't let them be afraid. You heard me tell you I am leaving, and I will come back to you.

"If you loved me, you would be happy that I am going to my Father because the Father is greater than I am. And I tell you this now before it happens, so when it does take place, you will be able to believe it. From now on I will not say many things to you. The prince of this world comes for me and has no power whatsoever over me. But so this world may know I love my Father, and—as he commanded me—I will obey."

The Savior said to us in this holy Gospel that "whoever loves me will keep my words." The test of love is doing good works. In other words, God wants us to act, so we can always honor him with our good works—not by naked words with no action—because love is shown through action.

"And my Father will love him. And we will come to him, and we will both live with him." The person who entertains these divine guests—not rejecting them with bad habits and black sins—will be happy. Nor do these divine guests come to visit without bringing the Love of both Father and Son, who is the Holy Spirit, sent on this same day to the apostles, and so God's Love was living with them. We know this to be true because the apostles, alive then on this earth, considered what God wanted and worked God's will. Their love for God was made manifest in good deeds. They did miracles and signs, ever strengthened through that same Spirit.

God tests every person's heart to determine whether he or she wants to enjoy God's indwelling presence or to love vices that displease God. And no one is ever rejected by God, unless that person has already decided to reject God's love for him. And then that person's sin is such that God will reject them because they have been careless about God's indwelling presence and apathetic towards his company.

The Savior said to us in this true Gospel, "Whoever does not love me will not keep my words." The love that loves God is not idle. Instead, it is strong and works great things always. And if love isn't willing to work, then it isn't love. God's love must be seen in the actions of our mouths and minds and bodies. A person must fulfill God's word with goodness.

"And the teaching you heard is not my word but comes from the same Father who sent me." The Savior, who said this, is called the *Word*, and he was born of the Father. And that is why Christ said the teaching he gave them was not his own word but his Father's because Christ is the Father's Word, and it was he who was then speaking with them about these truths. And common to them both are, without ambiguity, both words and works, and every good thing.

"I have spoken these things to you while I am still living with you." He was then living with them bodily, but even after he had quickly gone up from them to heaven, to the eternal joy he had always known, Christ lived with them through his divinity and always instructed them.

How? "The holy Spirit of Comfort whom my Father will send to you in my name will be the One teaching you all things and making everything I have said to you clear." The Holy Spirit is called *Paraclete* in the Greek language, and in Latin *Consolator*, which means "Comforter" in English. He is called these things because he comforts the hearts of those who repent of their sins. And by means of his great grace, God's Spirit forgives all the sins in all the world and makes anyone who trusts in God happy. And God's Spirit makes the heavenly angels rejoice together in God's Love always because God's Spirit is God's Love, of the Father and of the Son, common to them always, of them both ever, of one nature.

On this very day in a certain upper room, God's Spirit was sent then, as the Savior said, from the holy Father and also from his Son, and when he came, a loud heavenly sound covered the apostles like a fire, and in that house then there were one hundred and twenty of the Savior's followers, who served him in this world. They were the beginning of all Christianity, and through the great grace of the Holy Spirit they converted all the world to God. We have spoken more clearly about this event in another sermon for Pentecost, and by reading it or hearing it read aloud, a person can learn more about the Holy Spirit.

Ælfric's Sermons and Theology

If the Holy Spirit did not now illuminate your hearts with his spiritual grace, our words could not penetrate your hearts and stimulate your souls. And without the Holy Spirit's grace, our words couldn't help you improve your lives. And although you all hear this one reading, without a doubt each one of your hearts is not equally illuminated by this teaching because the Holy Spirit through his divinity gives his grace to you as he wishes. He is almighty God, and he holds all things with the Father and the Son in one divinity.

Then the Savior spoke these words to his apostles, "I leave you peace. I give you my peace." Christ always gave peace to his apostles, and he loves peace in those who believe in him, and also truth and honesty in everything. He left them in peace, and afterwards he gave them eternal peace in his heavenly kingdom with him.

"I do not give you the peace of this world." This world gives us transitory things, and Christ gives eternal things to those who love him.

"Don't let your hearts be anxious. Don't let them be afraid." The Savior comforted them with his cheerful words. He did not want them to be worried internally because of his imminent departure and journey to heaven.

And Christ spoke these words to them, as this Gospel tells us, "You heard me say now that I am leaving, and I will come back to you." He said this because he was leaving then and later would bring them to that place of eternal joy, as he had promised them.

"If you loved me, you would have rejoiced because I am going to my Father, because the Father is greater than I am." They loved Christ completely, but they were still afraid because he was so close to going away from them then to heaven. Still, they could rejoice in their hearts all the more because he journeyed up to glory, out of this conflict, and later they, too, would be permitted to follow him. With respect to the humanity of the Son, the Father is greater, and in this manner Christ spoke about these things before his passion, before he himself was glorified by his resurrection. That's why these words are well spoken about the humanity of Christ: Insofar as Christ is true God, he was always born of the almighty Father, just as mighty as he, because the Almighty cannot be less; and insofar as Christ was man, he was born of Mary; and insofar as Christ had a body, he lay buried; and insofar as Christ was dead, he rose up out of death, that is in the man (who could be dead) because his divine power could not be dead.

There was a certain proud heretic of old called Arrius. He wanted to belittle our dear Savior, saying he was weaker in his power than the holy Father was in his divinity. But Arrius's great sacrilege made this heretic experience a very embarrassing death, as books tell us. When Arrius went to the privy, his intestines fell out of him all at once. And this is the wretched manner in which he died, as empty on the inside as his faith. Why? In his folly Arrius had wanted to diminish the Savior's power, but the power of God's Son cannot be diminished.

Another heretic was called Olympius, and—because he was a heretic—he spoke nothing but the wickedness of untruths, heaping utter contempt on God's holy Trinity. But one day Olympius sat himself down in a bath, and fire came down on him there, suddenly and visibly, and burnt his body up entirely, as if it had been coals—so Olympius might know whom he censured. We must believe in the living Savior, that he is ever almighty God with the Father and with the Holy Spirit, in one godhead. That godhead can never be belittled.

This Gospel says further on that the Savior then said, "And I tell you this now before it happens, so when it does happen, you will be able to believe it." This is clearly spoken. And Christ continued, "From now on I will not say many things to you." Christ spoke these words to his disciples then because he would suffer the next morning for humanity and would no longer speak with them here in this world.

"The prince of this world comes for me and has no power whatsoever over me." That was the devil himself, who reigns over the sinful and is their evil prince. Satan came to the Savior and tried to discover if he could find any sin or some offense in Christ, but he found nothing, as the Savior said here in this Gospel you have just heard.

The devil lost all those of Adam's kin who believed in God. Although Satan had previously subjected them to his authority, Christ—the One who suffered guiltlessly and without sins—set them free and, victorious, journeyed away from hell with the spoil he had gotten there, all his chosen of Adam's family.

The Savior also spoke the words found at the end of this Gospel text, "But in order that this world may know I love my Father, and as he commanded me, I obey." We know Christ loved his Father because he was obedient to him unto death. And by obeying his Father's command, his Son set us free, though entirely voluntarily. To whom be glory forever with the Holy Spirit in eternity. Amen.

Introduction to Sermon XI

Sermon XI is unique in *God of Mercy* because it is the one true (in the modern sense of the word) 'sermon.' It does not explain a pericope of the day, as sermons I-X and XII-XVII do. These sixteen could, perhaps, be more properly referred to as 'homilies,' but the author, in an effort to keep terminology to a minimum, chose to follow the path set by Ælfric himself, who did not make fine distinctions between the two terms. Sermon XI is also the longest work here.

Instead of a pericope exegesis, sermon XI presents two subjects on which a lay congregation might need more information. The lyrical initial ninety-three lines summarize the principal events commemorated by the church between Christmas and Pentecost. These include Christ's nativity, crucifixion, resurrection, ascension, and his sending the Holy Spirit to his apostles, followed by a brief celebration of the Trinity. The remaining four-fifths and more (lines 94-574) is eschatological in nature. As Pope notes, these two parts fit together well—first Ælfric tells the Christian story, and then he spells out its eternal consequences.[1]

Ælfric begins the sermon by mentioning the Holy Spirit's seven gifts, a gentle reminder of their ability to empower a virtuous life and lead to an eternal one.[2] He concludes the sermon (and its long eschatological section) by affirming heaven's large, inclusive community and sole limitation—humanity's stubborn refusal to accept God's love: "Many people go from earth into heaven as God's saints because he wants to have a great crowd with him, as is very fitting."[3]

† † †

---

[1] Pope, *Homilies* I.407.
[2] Pope, *Homilies* I.418 (XI.68); cf. I.297 (V.208-13); I.384-85 (IX.121-49); and II.121-23 (XVII.572).
[3] Pope, *Homilies* I.445 (XI.545-47); see sermon II's introduction for a discussion of a similar passage.

Sermon XI

Sermon to the People, Delivered on the Octave of Pentecost

Today we want to explain the holy seasons that we faithfully observe in Christian churches and honor with God's songs of praise, so you can understand their meaning and know how the whole course of the year serves God Almighty. First, on Midwinter's Day we celebrate our Savior's nativity, how Christ came to us in true humanity and was invested with flesh for our deliverance, born of the holy virgin called Mary, she who alone is both virgin and mother.

On the twelfth day of that season, we celebrate with songs of praise the coming of the three faithful kings from the east, bringing gifts to Christ, and on that same day we celebrate the baptism of God's Son in the river Jordan by John the Baptist. Even though Christ was without sin, he was baptized because he wanted to hallow our baptism with his holy body and all streams of water by his going in for baptism.

On the fortieth day after Christ's nativity, which in English we call Candlemas, Christ's mother, the holy virgin Mary, carried the heavenly Prince to the holy temple with the sacrifices prescribed by the law, as the almighty God had commanded the great leader Moses in the earlier dispensation. And in the temple old Simeon gave God's Son his blessing and prophesied about him, and so did Anna the widow.

At the beginning of Lent we also celebrate with our songs of praise the beloved Savior's fasting forty days in the wilderness and overpowering the malicious devil who tempted there. Then at the latter part of Lent we celebrate in holy readings our Savior's passion. For our sins, Christ was fastened on the cross with four nails on Good Friday and was wounded with a spear after departing from this life and was buried that same day, and this is how he redeemed us with his own death.

Then Christ rose up out of death on Easter Sunday, and that same body in which he had suffered had been changed to an eternal body by means of immortality. And it is fitting that we celebrate this season by singing seven nights in a row as if they were one day because we are celebrating the great glory of humanity's redemption.

On the fortieth day after Christ rose up from death, and in the presence of his apostles who had followed him in this world, Christ ascended to his holy Father in heaven in the same body that he had raised from death. And it is fitting we celebrate that day on Thursday in the Rogation Week because through his own ascension (if we wish to earn it), Christ opened an ingress into heaven for us all.

Then, after ten nights from that time in our liturgy, we celebrate with great honor the day we call Pentecost, when the Holy Spirit came sounding out of heaven over the holy apostles in the likeness of a fire, filling the house where they were sitting and giving each of them so much power they were able to speak every language existing on earth. And the Holy Spirit also emboldened them for preaching the Gospel, so they went unafraid throughout this world converting heathens to the Savior's faith and working many miracles and baptizing people. For seven days we celebrate with our singing in church the holy coming of the Holy Spirit because of the seven gifts he gives to people. We told you before in another sermon how God's Spirit distributes gifts among Christians as he himself wishes because the Spirit is truly God.

This past week we have celebrated this season, and now today we praise the holy Trinity with our liturgy. And all during this week until Saturday night we will sing about that event, and with our songs of praise we will conclude the holy belief we have for God because we believe in the living God, in the holy Trinity who rules the heavens and also all created things from the beginning of the world, one almighty Creator, as writings and the holy fathers make known in Christian books.

Certainly God the Father was always with the Son, as was the Holy Spirit, throughout the entire course of the Son's life because they three are one God ruling heaven, ever reigning in one godhead, in one nature, all equally powerful. But the Son alone wholly took our humanity on himself, and that is how he saved us.

The entire liturgical year praises God Almighty and helps us observe the spiritual seasons, but we don't want to say any more about that now. Instead, we want to talk a little about ourselves. As we have often told you, the first created man, Adam our father, was so created by God that he could have always existed without sinning, and without death, if only he had obeyed his Lord. But if Adam sinned, he then became mortal. And he would have been happy had he not sinned, since he could certainly have refrained from sinning. But if Adam did sin, he then became a poor, unhappy man, since he could have stopped himself.

Then the old devil came, filled with hatred, and deceived Adam the first man and he sinned against God and broke his commandment. And then Adam became mortal, and all of his descendants, too. God did not create death, nor did he rejoice in humanity's ruin, as writings tell. *Inuidia autem diaboli mors intrauit in orbem terrarum*: "But through the devil's envy death came into this world." It comes in three ways, as is well known: *Mors acerba, mors immátura, mors naturalis.* In English that means, "Bitter death, premature death, and natural death." Bitter death is that which occurs to children. Premature death happens to young persons. And natural death comes to the old.

Every person dreads the death of the body, yet few dread the death of the soul. People work for the body (that cannot live long), yet they do not work for the soul that never dies in eternity. No evil death comes to those who have lived virtuously, but the person who pursued the way of death and pleased the devil with evil deeds will experience an evil death.

You don't need to wonder how death will come to you. You should be worried instead about how your soul will fare after death, according to your present deeds. It will go either to rest or to the worst punishments imaginable. These are the two deaths, as books tell us. One is the death of the body, coming to every person, and the other is the death of the soul, caused by sinning. The second death doesn't come to all people, only to those who are cruel. That person's soul is absent from eternal life and yet never dies in the hellish torments but is ever renewed to these, the eternal punishments. As our Lord said, those who keep his word escape this death, and they enjoy eternal life with the true Savior, whom they obeyed in this world.

God's friend is every person who is exceedingly quick to do good works to please God. These will come to the home promised to us. That home is the kingdom of heaven, as Christ promised us. Who could dare desire this delightful home and such great honor, if the benevolent Savior had not promised it to us? And Christ came to earth to redeem humanity—both men and women, and innocent children, and also monks and priests who preserve their purity and fight daily against Satan's temptations. God's promise cannot be denied to us, for he promised us the joy of the heavenly kingdom because of his mercy, not because of our goodness.

A great crowd of our faithful friends awaits our coming to them there in heaven. They are still solicitous about us, but they are free from care concerning themselves. They would like to see us living in that same happiness where they live. And who doesn't want to hurry now to that eternal haven, away from the difficulties in which we live and away from Satan's traps and to the merciful Lord? Still, those people who help many on earth must live among us as long as possible because they help us draw nearer to God.

The deceiving devil is always scheming against us, and even when a person is about to leave this life, Satan weaves many knots for him. That's why each person requires the many prayers of monks and priests. Everyone needs such intercession when earthly death draws near, so each person can escape this fiend. We read in books that the cruel devil came like a gruesome dragon to one prostrate young man. Satan wanted to own that young man's soul for hell because of his sins, but monks came to this man as he lay on his sickbed and earnestly prayed for him until they finally routed that fiendish dragon. And the young man got better, and he lived until he had atoned for his sins. And afterwards when he died, he did not see the dragon that time because it had been overpowered.

Someone must also administer the Eucharist to any sick person while they can still partake of it, before their last breath, because books tell us no one can take the Eucharist if they have already departed from this life. At the going forth of good people, God sends his angels to receive their souls at their going forth and to lead them to rest, as we learn in books. And Christ designates then for them the home they have earned here in this life. Those who are good and who pleased God on earth in all good works will live with God. And those who are not entirely good, not altogether cleansed from all their sins, will go to punishments and will suffer in these punishments until they become pure and are redeemed from that place through intercession.

The corrupt sinful people who obeyed Satan by sinning and despising their Lord, and so died, will go to hell as soon as they depart from life, and will always live there. However, if at the end of this life, when a person is sick, they should desire to turn to God and confess their sins with true repentance, the true Judge will have mercy on them, and they can with certainty escape from the devil on Doomsday.

The death that is common to all is not equally difficult for all people. To some, earthly death comes easily. But sometimes a sinful person will experience a difficult, tormenting death (or a fear of such a terrifying death) and will receive forgiveness of sins through that experience. Also, sometimes it also happens that certain people rejoice in their death and in their going forth, for they see for certain they will go to eternal rest, and their soul is glad, and departs happily from life.

According to the deeds done by people while alive, some souls journey to rest after their going forth; others go to punishments and are afterwards redeemed through alms deeds and especially through the Mass, if someone performs it on their behalf; and some are condemned with the devil to hell. And the person who arrives in hell never leaves it, and those who go to heavenly rest never go to the place of punishments.

As books tell us, in the afterlife, each soul possesses limbs like the body's and so perceives ease or pain—whichever it is in—according to what it merited before. Some sins are compensated for in this life and some after death, as our Lord said. But the great sins cannot be compensated for there, nor is it indeed helpful to the corrupt person for someone to perform Mass on their behalf, because they had not merited any of it before on earth.

Minor offenses and little sins are cleansed in the afterlife in that punishing fire of purgatory, and no king's punishment in this world is as severe as that fire that purges the careless. Some are there a long time, some a little while, depending on how a person's friends in this life act on his or her behalf, and according to what he or she merited before in this life.

And people can recognize each other there, too. And those who enter into rest absolutely recognize both those whom they knew before and those whom they did not know because they have all done good deeds and are therefore similar in soul. And the holy souls living in heaven pray both for us on earth and for the souls in purgatorial punishments. And they remember their faithful friends. And we can also intercede for those who are in purgatorial punishments, above all through the Mass, as books tell us. But no intercession helps those who are in hell.

Holy souls are very happy wearing the matchless apparel of eternal joy because in it they live without their bodies. But when Doomsday comes, through the power of their Lord, they will receive their body, though it had been rotted away. That's when they are adorned with beautiful bodies, which is the other robe of eternal joy. And then they are eternal, and ever immortal, both in soul and in body, happily with God. And their body is then very light and pleasant, though previously it had been heavy for them here on earth in this world. Daily they wish Doomsday would come quickly so they can rejoice in that double joy of soul and body. Still, they must wait on God's will for the time of reckoning and for the holy people of earth who will come to them then, until everyone is there who God intended when he first created this world.

Now they absolutely see the brightness of their Creator, and for that reason there is no created thing they are not able to see, both in heaven and on earth and in hell. But their happiness is not diminished by the fact that they see the sinful in punishments. Instead, they forever thank their Creator all the more for rescuing them from these fierce punishments. These holy souls clearly see all things, but sinful souls who live in torments cannot know what happens to us. Still, they feel concern for their friends here in this world, but their concern does not help their friends or them one bit.

As the Savior said, no person living or dead, nor any created thing knows when the great Judgment shall come to all people, because God himself created all things as he wished, asking no one else's opinion. Also, the day of this world's end does not come as the result of any person's decision but only through the foresight of the One who created all things.

About that day of Judgment, our Savior himself said people will build and go about their business, and men will take wives, and women will take husbands, until that great day comes to all people. And the Savior himself will come with his shining angels, and both the sun and the moon will grow dark because of the enormous light of the mighty Lord.

Now understand, people, how much power exists in Christ, when the sun and the moon cannot give any light because of the divine light that emanates from the Savior. Hosts of angels will bear the bright cross before him. And Christ's murderers will see the One whom they killed before, and he will explicitly show his wounds to them. Then the sinful will weep and greatly grieve, those who despised the Savior here in this world. They will acknowledge their sins with sad hearts. Then one fire will cover all this world. And the angel will blow the seventh trumpet—the last one—and everyone will rise up who had existed in this world in living bodies. And at that time the living who come from hell will be there just as soon as the living who are found alive in this world.

The living will be slain by that fire immediately, but right afterwards they will be revived in an eternal body, like the others. And then—whether they died in old age or in childhood—they will all be the same age afterwards, which is the age of Christ when he suffered. Every person will still have his own stature, though. Each person will either be the size they were before as a person on earth, or, if they departed from life as children or half-grown adults, they will be the size they would have possessed had they grown to maturity.

So God created both men and women in soul and body, and made them humans, and then afterwards he redeemed both sexes; and God will also raise them out of death on Doomsday, both men and women. And they will live forever as two sexes, but without any lust, either good or evil. And afterwards no man will ever take a wife, nor will a woman take a husband, nor will they have children.

The saints who go to heaven are also not hurt in any way, nor are they sick, or one-eyed. Even though one of them might have been lame on earth, all their limbs will then be sound, in shining brightness, and solid in the spiritual body. But the cruel person will always live in pain. Is there any sort of brightness destined for him in that black fire, where there is only grief and terrible teeth grinding? And those in hell want to disappear and become nothing or be dead, but they must remain where they are, for they can never be delivered from hell's painful punishment.

At the time of the last trumpet, every person who ever existed in this world will rise up. If someone drowned or was eaten by wild animals or was burned up suddenly by fire, becoming dust, and that dust was scattered by blasts of wind, nevertheless almighty God can raise that person again because God made this world out of nothing. And the belief of the person who does not believe this is nothing. As custom dictates, a dead person is wrapped with a robe, but that robe does not then more readily rise with the person at the sound of the trumpet because no one has need of a transitory earthly robe then, but of the spiritual garments preordained by God.

Then God will send his angels, and they will gather to him all his chosen ones from every part of the world. And the good people will stand at God's right hand and the wicked at his left. The Savior will then sit in his heavenly seat of majesty, mighty and full of glory, where he is mild to the good and terrifying and terrible to poor sinful ones. And all people will clearly see the Savior in his humanity; however, those poor sinful people will not be permitted to see his divinity. Only the good will see Christ's divinity.

The twelve apostles who followed Christ in this world will also sit then in twelve judgment seats, and the holy people who rejected this world, despising earthly goods altogether, will sit on judgment seats with them. And then with the Savior they will judge humanity.

Four groups of people make up that great crowd. The first group is the one just mentioned, who sit with the Savior in their judgment seats. They won't be judged, but with Christ in glory they will mightily judge all other people. The second group consists of those who pleased God earlier with their good works, and with alms deeds they merited from God the heavenly home and eternal glory. They will not judge anyone, but they will be judged and will come to possess the glory of the heavenly kingdom.

Then the third group is made up of the Christian people who were acquainted with their belief but who provoked God with their cruel deeds. They lived constantly and completely in unkind sins. They were evil murderers, greedy misers, wizards and witches, makers of poisons, thieves and robbers, savage sorcerers, perjurors, deceitful violators of agreements, betrayers in marriage, and vile prostitutes who kill their children before they are born. They did no good as honor to God and no almsgiving, but ended in sins. They are then doomed along with the devil to hell.

The fourth group is made up of sinful heathens who had no friendly relations with the heavenly God, nor did they know the faith of Christ in their lives. They spent their time on earth in the practices of the devil and always sinned against God's law. And afterwards they will perish in eternity without God's law, always suffering along with those who believe wrongly.

At that time no one can hide anywhere, but all people who were ever alive are present there. And all our thoughts and all our deeds will be revealed there to all the crowds. Sins that had been compensated for at an earlier time will not be revealed, but unexpiated sins will be manifested there. Those people who did not want to confess their sins earlier and did not want to do penance according to their teacher's direction will then be put to shame and will grieve. At the right Judgment all are equal, both lord and slave, rich and poor, and no person can have a witness there testifying for them because all deeds will be made public to everyone there.

Then the Savior will speak from his holy seat of majesty to those who believed and performed God's will and who stand at his right side. Christ will say to them, *Uenite, benedicti Patris mei, Et cetera*: "'Come, you blessed of my heavenly Father, and receive the kingdom prepared for you from the very beginning of this world. I hungered terribly, and you fed me. Then, when I was thirsty, you gave me drink. And I was also a stranger, and you accepted me. I was naked, and you clothed me. I was also sick, and you visited me. I was in prison, and you came to see me.'

"Then they will answer the merciful Judge, saying, 'Dear Lord, when did we see you hungry and fed you, or thirsty and gave you drink? And when were you a stranger and we received you, or when were you naked and we clothed you? When were you sick and we visited you, or in prison and we came to see you?'

"Then the King will answer these good people, saying, 'I tell you the truth, you did these kindnesses to me any time you did them to any one of these little brothers or sisters of mine.'" We should surely understand this to mean—as often as you gave alms to one little beggar among those who believe, you gave it to Christ because Christ is the head of Christians. And those who believe in God are Christ's limbs.

"Then the Judge will afterwards say to the sad crowd who stand at his left, 'Go away, you who are damned, into the eternal fire prepared for the devil and his angels. I hungered terribly, and you didn't feed me. And I was thirsty, and you didn't give me drink. I was a stranger, and you did not take me in. I was also naked, and you weren't willing to clothe me. I was sick and in prison, and you didn't come see me.'

"Then the sinful will answer the true Judge, saying, 'True Lord, when did we see you hungry or thirsty, a stranger or naked, sick or in prison, and did not minister to you?' Then the Judge will answer the poor guilty ones, 'I tell you the truth, you denied me all these things as often as you denied them to one of these little ones.'"

Then these poor, wretched sinful people will enter the eternal punishment to live with the damned devil, while the righteous will accompany the Savior to eternal life, with his crowds of angels. These words of Jesus help us know that without a doubt are the sinful first made to sink into hell along with the damned devils, where they must live, and then afterwards the saints make their journey to heaven.

Concerning this same sequence of events, John also wrote this: "Each one of them was judged according to his own works, and then death and hell entered the enormous sea of crackling fire." This death and this hell is the devil himself because he is the prince of eternal death and the origin of all the punishments of those judged sinful and unrepentant.

John also said this about these unrepentant people: "Every person whose name is not already written down in that living book of the eternal memory will be thrown into this enormous fiery sea. The names of the saints who live with the Savior have been written down in that glorious book. That is the predestination existing from the beginning with God." In this blazing fiery sea burn pitiable humans and proud devils, together. That fire is also eternal, and so they burn eternally. But their bodies can never burn up because their bodies are eternal after the resurrection.

Now some people ponder how the unblessed devils can feel the burning of that fire on them there, since they are spirits and do not have bodies. Now we tell as truth that the soul of a person is imprisoned in his body while he is living, and it cannot leave the body when and as it wishes. On earth a person's soul must endure in that body, for better or worse, in joy and pain, and then, when the soul is outside of the body, the body feels no pain. Just as easily can almighty God imprison the devils in that dark fire so that they suffer in its heat and cannot escape. And the One who gladdens the holy angels in heaven can also afflict the devils in that fire, though they are spirits who are fully condemned.

The punishment of humanity is so meted out by God that the person who sinned less will suffer less, and the person who sinned more will suffer more. And each person suffers there as they deserve. The gentlest punishment and the lightest is for the innocent children who were unbaptized, who performed no other sin through themselves except the one Adam perpetrated. And through that one sin all humanity was brought to ruin, except those who believed in the living Savior and were baptized with regard to this earlier sin. After the condemned persons and the devils have been brought into the enormous fire, neither can see the joy the saints experience. But, confined there, they suffer throughout eternity.

John the Evangelist, in his spiritual sight, said that subsequent to this he saw an entirely new heaven and a new earth because this earth will be fully renewed by the huge fire appearing so suddenly at Christ's coming, and also the sun and certainly the moon will be seven times brighter than they are now, as books tell us. And the new heaven and new earth are peopled solely by the chosen ones of God, who prepared many rooms for his saints.

After this Judgment our Lord will go to his heavenly Father with the holy people whom he raised on earth from dust and will commit them to his Father, as it says in books, *Cum tradiderit regnum Patri suo*. In our English language that means, "Then he will commit the kingdom to his Father" because they are the kingdom of God, and they reign with God. Then Christ will grant them what he promised them in this world when he called from the earth to his almighty Father: "My Father, I desire that these whom you gave me out of this earth may live with me where I myself am, so they may see my brightness that you gave me because you loved me before the world came into being."

The Savior is absolutely the head of his saints, and they reign with him, like his angels. And they see God as clearly as angels do, as John said to those who believe in Christ, "We will certainly see him clearly as he is." And the apostle Paul also said in his epistle, "Now we see as if through a looking glass, and in a riddle, but afterwards in eternal life we will see God face to face." Again the Savior said in his holy Gospel, "Where I myself am, there is my servant, and the person who serves me honors my Father."

Many people go from earth into heaven as God's saints because he wants to have a great crowd with him, as is very fitting. And they are all ordered as they deserve. According to how they loved their Creator on earth, they are also glorified in that great honor. And there is no envy in any one of them, but they all exist in one fellowship and are always living in true peace. And there in heaven the person who seemed in this world to be the least significant is very great and very famous in glory. And this person wants no more glory than that which can be enjoyed through the Savior's grace.

In heaven, everyone can read everyone else's thoughts. Also, no one is ever hungry there, nor depressed, nor thirsty, nor sick in any way. Instead, they all live in harmony with Christ, loving him without ceasing and praising him without growing weary. And Christ himself is then everything to them all, and they lack nothing, since they have him. He is their kingdom and life, their honor and salvation and glory, peace and abundance. And heaven is the place where the eternal day never ends, and God's will will then be doubly glorified in soul and body. And they will always shine as bright as the sun in the kingdom of their Father, who lives and reigns with his beloved Son and with the Holy Spirit, in one godhead, one almighty God, forever. Amen.

Introduction to Sermon XII

Sermon XII was likely completed during the middle of Ælfric's monkhood, between *Lives of Saints* (998) and the start of his Eynsham abbacy in 1005.[1] At lines 156-58, Ælfric is inspired by Augustine's twelfth tractate to create a particularly beautiful Old English passage with striking threefold repetition: "Where someone sings God's praises, the sound of the Spirit's voice is heard. Where someone speaks God's teaching, the sound of the Spirit's voice is heard. Where someone meditates on God, the Spirit's grace is found." As Pope points out, this passage gives "emotional force and a sense of progression to three successive aspects of Christian worship: the sounding of the psalms, of the gospel, of the divine word itself."[2] Sermon XII concludes with a fine example of Old English typology: "The brass serpent, which was without poison, prefigured the death of Christ, who suffered without sin, lifted up on the cross."[3]

---

[1] Pope, *Homilies* I.332. See the introductions to sermons VII, VIII, IX, and X.
[2] Pope, *Homilies* I.478.
[3] Pope, *Homilies* I.489 (XII.230-32).

Sermon XII

For the First Sunday after Pentecost
John 3.1-15

"There was a certain Pharisee named Nicodemus, one of the rulers of the Jewish people. One night he came to the Savior and said: 'We know, dear teacher, that you come from God. Obviously no one can work such miracles as you do, unless God is with him.' The Savior answered him, saying, 'I tell you the truth, no one ever sees the kingdom of God, unless he is born again.'

"This astonished Nicodemus, and he said to Jesus, 'How can a grown man be born again? Can he, indeed, go back into his mother's womb, and be born again like that?' But the Savior said to him, 'I tell you the truth, whoever is not born again of water and the Holy Spirit cannot enter the kingdom of God. Whatever is born of flesh is surely flesh, and whatever is born of spirit is surely spirit. Don't be astonished that I have now told you it is necessary for you to be born again. The Spirit breathes intimately wherever he wishes, and you hear his voice, but still you don't know where the Spirit comes from, or where he goes. Every person who is born of the spirit is just like that.'

"Nicodemus said to Jesus, 'How can these things be?' The Savior answered him again, saying, 'You are a distinguished teacher among Israel's people, and yet you don't know these things?' And Christ said to him again, 'I tell you the truth, we absolutely speak what we know for certain, and we also affirm what we have seen; yet you are in no way willing to receive our testimony among you. If I openly tell you about earthly things and you don't believe them, how then will you believe me if I want to tell you about heavenly things? And no one ascends to heaven at all, except him who descended down from heaven to here. That is the Son of Man, he who is in heaven. And so Moses in the great wilderness lifted up the serpent as a sublime sign, as it is fitting to lift up the Son of Man in some high place, so the ones who believe in Christ will not be lost, but will have eternal life for themselves.'"

The holy Gospel we heard now has great significance, but we must speak to you in keeping with your understanding so you won't be entirely deprived of the teaching, nor of our Lord's words. The Pharisee called Nicodemus drew near to Christ at night wanting to hear his holy teaching, though notice he came secretly at night. Nicodemus didn't dare come to the

Lord during the day because the Jews had audaciously outlawed everyone who believed in him.

Nicodemus was one of the rulers of the chief councillors of the Jewish people, and he went at night to speak with the Savior. And Nicodemus spoke these words to Christ then: "We know, dear teacher, that you come from God. No one can genuinely work such miracles as you do, unless God is with him." Nicodemus was wise and understood the Savior's miracles and the great power Christ exercised among humanity because Jesus healed all the infirmities of everyone who came to him.

And then Nicodemus said to Jesus that he had come from God and that God was with him and that he wanted to learn his teaching from him secretly at night because he did not dare do so during the day. The Savior answered him, saying, "I tell you the truth, no one ever sees the kingdom of God, unless he is born again." Nicodemus came at night to Christ, and the night signified Nicodemus's ignorance. He did not yet know that the other birth Christ spoke about was the holy baptism Christ himself established, in which all people are cleansed from sins.

And Nicodemus said in his ignorance then, "How can a grown man be born again? Can he go back into his mother's womb and be born again like that?" These words spoken by Nicodemus in his ignorance to Christ have a certain signification, as this sermon tells us. In his ignorance, Nicodemus said that that birth which is well known to us all cannot be repeated in life. In other words, a person cannot be born a second time from his mother. These words signify much concerning the spiritual birth of a person into God's church: It cannot be repeated. In other words, a person cannot receive baptism two times. Even if a Mass priest who is wicked baptizes a child in the true belief of the holy Trinity, that child must not be baptized again by a better teacher because the holy Trinity must not be dishonored. Nor can an evil priest's own sins defile God's ministry that comes from God himself because in that true baptism the Holy Spirit washes a heathen person clean of all sins.

But the Savior said to him, "I tell you the truth, whoever is not born again of water and the Holy Spirit cannot enter into the kingdom of God." This was immediately made clear at the very beginning of the world, when God first created all things through his might: "Then the very Spirit of God was," as the book tells us, "moving over the waters," so our baptism was even then prefigured with coming power, and the nature of water was hallowed through the Holy Spirit, who hallows our baptism and washes the soul within from every sin.

Now you shouldn't keep your children too long heathen because it is dangerous for them, for they cannot enter heaven if they die heathen. Remember, they will not be children on Doomsday. They will then be as big as they might have been if they had grown to maturity at the usual age. And the heathen child lives in hell forever, and the baptized go to heaven, in body and soul, and they both live forever, with no end.

"That which is born of flesh is surely flesh, and that which is born of spirit is surely spirit." The spiritual birth is unseen, and the birth of the body is fully seen, since a child grows up and then becomes a boy and later is a young man, until in this way he reaches the age that his Creator grants him. The spiritual birth—when a person is born by God in holy baptism through the Holy Spirit—is unseen to us because we cannot see what is performed there in the baptized person. You see him dipped into the clear water and then lifted up out of it, and he looks just as he did before he was immersed.

But the Holy Mother, who is God's church, knows that a child is dipped, sinful, into the font, and is drawn up cleansed from sins through holy baptism. Through Adam's transgression, which broke God's command, children are sinful, but through the grace of God himself their sins are destroyed, so that they are people of God. And from the fleshly nature the spiritual nature comes into being and is called "the child of God," as books tell us.

Later, the Savior spoke these words to Nicodemus, "Don't be astonished that I have now told you it is necessary for you to be born again." He wanted him to know the spiritual birth, without which Nicodemus could not be Christ's follower. And Christ urged him towards that birth by using obscure words, which afterwards Jesus revealed to us.

"The Spirit breathes intimately where he wants to, and you hear his voice, but you don't know where the Spirit comes from, or where he goes. Every person who is born of the Spirit is just like that." The Holy Spirit breathes where he wants to because he has the power to illuminate the mind of anyone he wishes and convert it to good, from foolishness to wisdom, from error to belief, from the performance of sins to true penance. God's Holy Spirit can turn anyone's mind away from all perversities and to that which is right.

Where someone sings God's praises, the sound of the Spirit's voice is heard. Where someone speaks God's teaching, the sound of the Spirit's voice is heard. Where someone meditates on God, the Spirit's grace is found. But you cannot see how that very same Spirit comes into the good person who receives God's Spirit, even if you look on him and hear his teaching. Why? It's because the nature of the Spirit is unseen. And that person becomes a different person, transformed from evil to a better will through the grace of the Spirit.

Nicodemus said to Christ, "How can these things be?" The Savior answered him again, saying, "You are a teacher in Israel, and yet you do not know this?" The Savior did not say this—*Are you a teacher and yet you do not know this mystery*—to reproach Nicodemus. No, Christ wanted instead to bring about in Nicodemus the improvements only true humility can accomplish. Without humility no person can thrive in the Lord.

And later Christ said to him, as this Gospel tells us, "I tell you the truth, we speak what we know for certain, and we also affirm what we have seen, and yet you are in no way willing to receive our testimony among you." The Savior told him what he himself knew to be true. And also Christ's affirmation of these truths that he himself had witnessed proved their validity, even though some Jews didn't want to accept his teaching or his affirmation or Christ himself as a guide. But many people throughout the world did honestly receive the faith of the Savior and his teaching, and until this world ends many will continue to accept him.

"If I openly tell you about earthly things and you do not believe them, how then can you believe me if I want to tell you about heavenly things?" Christ told the Jews about earthly things when he told them of his passion and the resurrection of his own body that he had accepted from earth of an earthly mother.

And here Christ spoke about heavenly things when he spoke of baptism and when he then spoke of his ascension to heaven and eternal life, that is certainly divine. And the unblessed did not believe what he said.

"And no one ascends to heaven, except the One who descended from heaven to here. That is the Son of Man who is in heaven." The Savior is surely the Son of one Man, as none other is. And he is our Head. And Christ descended from heaven to deliver us, and then he ascended after his passion. And he promised his saints that they would be permitted to follow him and to live with him where he himself lives. Then he ascended alone, but his own limbs followed after him, up to the Head. And God's saints, who are Christ's limbs on earth, will always follow him there until the end of this world. God's saints always go from here to him, from this transitory life to their dear Lord, until they are all gathered to the Head.

Christ's human nature did not come with him out of heaven, nor was it in heaven when Christ said this, but Christ is one Savior in each nature,

God's and man's, and that is why it was fitting for Christ to speak to Nicodemus as you heard in this reading—when Christ said that he descended from heaven and had been in heaven.

"And so Moses in the great wilderness lifted up the serpent as a sublime sign, as it is fitting to lift up the Son of Man in some high place, so the ones who believe in Christ won't be lost but will have eternal life for themselves." We have given the interpretation for this passage very clearly in two other sermons, but we still want to explain this conclusion to you briefly.

In the great wilderness, when the nation was bitten by the serpents, Moses the leader made one brass serpent as God commanded. And then he raised up the brass serpent as a sign, and those who had been bitten there looked at it. And immediately they got better. The brass serpent, which was without poison, prefigured the death of Christ, who suffered without sin, lifted up on the cross. And we look to Christ with full belief, and through him we will be delivered from our sins and will always have life with him in eternity, as Christ promised us. To God's Son is ever honor and glory forever with his heavenly Father and with the Holy Spirit, in one godhead. We say Amen.

Introduction to Sermon XIII

Sermon XIII exegetes Luke 6.36-42, giving Ælfric the opportunity to talk at length on social justice:

> Christ commanded us to be kind to others always, with all goodness, just as God himself is, but the person who causes others stress is not being kind. Instead, without hesitation the unmerciful pile heavy burdens on the backs of those they know. And they are always mean. It's very unfair that cruel people rob the poor; and yet see how they dare desire a life of luxury for themselves, though they are never willing to acknowledge their oppression of the poor. Bosses who cannot permit those working under them to know kindness during this life of labor should never themselves enjoy lives of luxury because they could easily be kind to their workers every day. And then they would have some kindness in their souls. God loves kindness. God loves it when a person is gentle towards others in the daily hardships all humanity must endure and in the many heavy taxes and in the unending laws. And God detests those who oppress others. But God loves those who are kind and merciful to others.[1]

Sermons XIII, XIV, XV, and XVI were written for the fifth, sixth, seventh, and tenth Sundays after Pentecost, filling in gaps in the Sundays found in Ælfric's two-volume *Catholic Homilies*. They were most likely finished towards the end of Ælfric's career, sometime during his service as abbot of Eynsham; their accomplished style and freedom in dealing with sources accord with a late composition date. Sermons XIII and XV share an emphasis on God's mercy and may have been written as a complementary pair.[2] One of Ælfric's main sources here seems to be Bede's commentary on Luke; the very effective exemplum closing the sermon (the story of Jesus and the woman taken in adultery, John 8.1-11) is an addition Ælfric makes to his source material.[3]

☩ ☩ ☩

---

[1] Pope, *Homilies* II.499-500 (XIII.54-71).
[2] Pope, *Homilies* II.493.
[3] Pope, *Homilies*, II.494, 496.

Sermon XIII

For the Fifth Sunday after Pentecost
Luke 6.36-42

Luke the Evangelist, who was a physician in life, healed many people from various diseases by his skill in doctoring, but through his teaching he has cured the souls of many more people eternally. Luke wrote down about the Savior that on one occasion while here in this world Christ spoke these words in his Gospel to his holy apostles, and through them to us, *Estote ergo misericordes, et reliqua*: "'So be merciful, just as your Father is. Don't judge at all, and you will not be judged. Don't condemn, and you will not be condemned. Forgive other people, and you will be forgiven. Give alms and do good, and good will be given to you. However much you now give, God will give back into your lap abundantly, completely full and shaken down and even overflowing, as your reward. The measure you use to give good to others will be the one used to measure out good back to you.'

"He also honestly told them this parable in these words: 'How can the blind lead the blind? Won't they not both fall into a dark pit? The disciple cannot be ahead of his teacher. Every one of them is complete who is like his teacher. Why, how can you for certain see that speck in your brother's eye, and yet you can't see the beam in your own eye? And how can you say these words to your brother: 'My brother, let me draw that speck out of your eye,' and yet you yourself are unwilling to see the beam in your own eye? Instead, hypocrite, first pull out the beam from your eye, and only then look to pull out the speck from your brother's eye.'"

To those who have not been taught well, these are strange words. Now we want to reveal their meaning to you and more clearly explain their significance. In this holy Gospel the Savior commanded us, "So be merciful, just as your Father is." Here you are able to learn about the Savior's goodness because he himself spoke these words about us. If we will behave in a merciful manner, we ourselves will be permitted to have such a Father, even that heavenly God, because God is merciful. Notice that God lets his sun shine both on good people and on evil people. Notice that God sends showers of rain to the righteous and to the unrighteous. Notice that God gives earthly fruits as food to all people, to those who love him and to those who hate him. Notice that even when a person hates his Creator and neglects his commands and doesn't fulfill God's words with good deeds, that the heavenly Father still feeds him, so at some time this person may turn to God. Or else at his death this person will rightly be delivered to the cruel devil, if he does not turn to God before that time.

Christ commanded us to be kind to others always, with all goodness, just as God himself is, but the person who causes others stress is not being kind. Instead, without hesitation the unmerciful pile heavy burdens on the backs of those they know. And they are always mean. It's very unfair that cruel people rob the poor; and yet see how they dare desire a life of luxury for themselves, though they are never willing to acknowledge their oppression of the poor. Bosses who cannot permit those working under them to know kindness during this life of labor should never themselves enjoy lives of luxury because they could easily be kind to their workers every day. And then they would have some kindness in their souls.

God loves kindness. God loves it when a person is gentle towards others in the daily hardships all humanity must endure and in the many heavy taxes and in the unending laws. And God detests those who oppress others. But God loves those who are kind and merciful to others. The prophet spoke these words about God's mercy, *Misericordiam et iudicium cantabo tibi, Domine*: "I sing to you, LORD, about true mercy and the very just judgment with which you judge humanity." The prophet said this because God is merciful to people here in this world, so they may turn from their sins to him. And on those who foolishly scorn him, God will pronounce judgment in the life that is to come—that life they now show little regard for—because now is the time in which God is merciful, and when the End comes, that is the time for God to judge all.

God is very merciful to those who place their hope in him. He is especially merciful to those who are kind and right-minded and who refuse to participate in the unfair oppression of others. These people only disturb others for righteous correction and good laws.

The Gospel goes on to speak these words in this order: "Don't judge, and you will not be judged." Christ did not altogether forbid every judgment by the elders, by those who ought to judge. Instead, he banned presumptuousness. He wants us always to find out first what is right.

Certain things are now secret that God himself will judge later. And other things are public, and judgment must be given on these matters. For example, no one should willingly defend a guilty person. No one should deceive an innocent person and bring them to ruin. No one should take a bribe to deny what is true. No one should let fear make them trumpet what is false.

Instead, with mercy everyone should direct others rightly, as this Gospel says next: "Condemn no one, and you will not be condemned." James the Just wrote down in his epistle that judgment without mercy will be reserved for the person who now judges others without mercy. "Forgive other people, and you will be forgiven." God commands us to forgive the injuries done to us by others. Why? Through the forgiveness we have for others, God forgives us our own sins.

"Give alms and do good, and good will be given to you." God increases the possessions of the person who gives alms for him, and God repays him one hundred times more than whatever he gave in alms.

"However much you now give, God will give back into your lap abundantly, completely full and shaken down and even overflowing, as your reward." This does not mean that the poor people we help will later pay us back for whatever we gave them. Instead, God himself very gladly pays us back on their behalf for everything we now do for them in his name for a good end, so our reward is abundant and overflowing on every side.

"The measure you use to give good to others will be the one used to measure out good back to you." This saying applies to all of our deeds, both words and actions. On the day of Judgment, God rewards every person according to their good deeds on earth.

"He also honestly told them this parable in these words: 'How can the blind lead the blind? Won't they both fall into a dark pit?'" A parable in the Gospels frequently says one thing but means something else entirely. Only a knowledgeable teacher can guide unlearned laypersons to God's righteousness. Anyone who wants to correct the sins of a foolish person must first stop his or her own evil habits. A teacher must always present the unlearned with a virtuous example.

"The disciple cannot be ahead of his teacher. Every one of them is complete who is like his teacher." Christ himself is the Teacher, and he gave us the example of being merciful to others in the same way he is merciful to us. And there is no way we can live on this earth without facing hardship and persecution because our teacher himself faced these. But we should endure much for Christ's sake, just as he taught us by example. Many a young student often realizes that in time his intellect has surpassed that of the teacher who instructed him from his earliest years. And for that reason the omniscient Savior is mentioned here as Teacher because we will become perfect in love if we follow his example.

"Tell me, how can you for see with confidence that speck in your brother's eye, and yet you can't see the beam in your own eye? And how can you say to your brother: 'Brother, let me draw that speck out of your eye,' and yet you yourself are unwilling to see the beam in your own eye?" A long beam cannot literally lie in your eye, but this beam signifies the meanness of hatred. It symbolizes the hostile heart that hates.

And the speck signifies the anger of someone you know. Obviously you can't see to pull a speck out of someone else's eye unless first you get rid of the hatred in yourself. Hatred is a capital sin. And then after you have corrected yourself, then and only then can you correct the other person's anger. But if you hate someone, you cannot correct that person.

Christ meant the same thing when he said elsewhere, *Liquantes culicem et glutientes camelum*: "They use a sieve to strain a gnat out of their drink, but they swallow a camel whole." He means that they censure little sins with a hateful spirit and pride—the greatest sin—as if they were straining out a gnat, but they are not willing to reform the great sins in themselves. Instead, they give in to the sin of scorn and perversely desire only to enjoy condemning others' wrongs, while all the time they possess more sinfulness than those they reprimand.

"Instead, you hypocrite, first pull the beam from your eye, and then you can see to draw the speck from your brother's eye." A hypocrite is a person who thinks he should put someone else right before he puts himself right. A hypocrite acts as if he eschews sins, and yet he is full of them. But Christ—who overlooked nothing—instructed us and then commanded us above all things to root out our hidden vices and evil hatred. After these are removed from our hearts, only then can a person with a pure heart put right the insignificant sins in other people.

Certain people should correct others. The sagacious to whom God gives wisdom and authority must correct others, but they must always do so with gentleness and great love. And they must never forget their own vices, so God can be praised in his holy followers.

We want to tell you a certain exemplum showing how the Savior himself behaved in this world: "Christ came to the hill called the Mount of Olives, beside the city of Jerusalem, in the land of the Jews. Then at daybreak he walked into the temple, and all of the people immediately thronged in to him. And he sat himself down and taught them eagerly, as was his custom. And on that day the Pharisees and scribes brought a woman into the temple. And she had been caught in the wickedness of adultery. And they thrust her in front of him, saying: 'You beloved Teacher, this woman has been seized in public fornication, and in Moses's law it was surely commanded that such a guilty woman must be condemned to death by stoning. What do you have to say to us about such a deed?'

"They said this to him to tempt him, so they could accuse his teaching." If Christ chose to save the life of this adulterous woman, then through his kindness he would be breaking their law, and if Christ commanded that that woman be stoned to death, then he would become cruel in their sight.

"He then stooped down and wrote on the ground with his finger, and they continued to ask him what he would do. Then the Savior sat up and said these words to them: 'Whichever one of you has no sin in him should cast the first stone at her then.' And then he wrote some more on the ground. And when they had heard this, the leaders left one by one, and the woman was left alone, standing before the Savior.

"He then sat up again and said to the woman: 'Why, woman, where are your loud accusers? Has none of them condemned you to death for that?' Frightened, the woman answered him, 'No, dear Lord, not one of them condemned me.' The Savior said to her: 'Nor do I condemn you. You can go ahead and leave, and from now on, don't sin.' "

That's how Christ forgave this woman's guilt. He told her that from that day on she should control herself and no longer practice adultery because every person who confesses their sins and then does the same things against our Lord, insults Christ and is like the dog who eats its vomit. That person is also like a pig who rolls in the muck after a bath. And that person's end will be worse than his or her beginning.

May the Savior ever direct us to his will, to whom is glory and praise forever. Amen.

Introduction to Sermon XIV

Sermon XIV may have been written as late as 1009 or 1010, making it potentially the latest sermon translated in *God of Mercy*.[1] It contains Ælfric's most severe denunciation of English sinfulness, at lines 98-107 and 132-39.[2] In the second of these two passages, he criticizes the English who submit to the Danes. Ælfric may be referring to defections occurring over a period of years; these started in 992 with Ealdorman Ælfric's disloyalty as reported by the Chronicle and were followed in 994 by an Essex conspiracy accepting the Danish Swein as king. It is reasonable to assume both Wulfstan (in *Sermo Lupi Ad Anglos*) and Ælfric (here in XIV) did not write about these defections until the situation had reached alarming proportions.[3]

The Vikings ravaged the countryside near Eynsham near the end of 1006, when Ælfric may have witnessed many local examples of disloyalty. After a two-year hiatus, the Vikings returned in 1009, when Wulfnoth of Sussex led some twenty British ships into piracy; and the Chronicle entry for 1010 records mass defections that marked the widespread English demoralization towards the end of Ethelred II's disastrous thirty-eight-year reign (978–1016).[4] Ethelred's infamous kingship, torn by dissension within and wrecked by Danes from without, earned him the sobriquet, 'Ethelred the Unready,' from the Old English *Unræd*, literally meaning, 'without good counsel.'

---

[1]Pope, *Homilies* I.148-9 and II.493.
[2]Pope, *Homilies*, II.512-14.
[3]Pope, *Homilies* II.513.
[4]Pope, *Homilies* II.513-14.

Sermon XIV

For the Sixth Sunday after Pentecost
Luke 5.1-11

"Long ago, when the Savior was living in this world among humanity, one day he stood with some people beside a fishing ground. That fishing ground was a large lake called Gennesaret. And the many people ran to him and wanted to hear his holy teaching. And Christ saw two ships standing beside the lake, and the fishermen among them who fished in the lake had come out of the water and were washing their nets.

"Peter was then a fisherman, who is now an apostle. His ship stood near Jesus. The Savior climbed into it and commanded Peter to push his ship a little away from the land. And then Christ sat down in the ship near the land and taught the people who stood on the shore, as was his custom. Then after teaching them, Christ commanded the holy Peter to let his ship go out into the deep, and he commanded them to cast out their nets into the fishing ground.

"Peter answered him: 'Dear teacher, we have worked all night, staying awake but without success, for we caught not one fish. But at your word I will now cast out the net.' And then they cast it out, and the net immediately became filled with fishes until it began bursting, but they motioned immediately to their companions on the other ship, to come quickly and help them. They came at once, and both ships filled with fishes until they nearly sank.

"When Peter saw such a catch of fish, then immediately he fell at the Savior's knees and humbly said to him, awed: 'Depart from me, Lord, for I am a sinful man.' He was terrified, and so were his companions; and even James and John, the sons of Zebedee, were frightened by that catch of fishes.

"Then the Savior spoke these words to holy Peter: 'Don't fear anything because of this event. From now on you will catch men as you caught fishes.' Then they rowed their heavy ships to land and left all things to follow Christ."

This fishing ground was very beautiful to look at and was located in the land of the Jews, in the Galilean district. And it was a very large freshwater lake, many miles long and three miles wide. Water flows solely out of the great river men call Jordan and into that lake. The fishing there is splendid. And men called it "Sea" because this body of water was so huge.

"The Savior then stood beside that lake with the people, and the people drew near him to hear his teaching" because people of all nations now run to him, in true belief, seeking his teaching. The two ships that Christ saw standing there signify the people in the land of the Jews who believed in the holy Savior and also the Gentile people who from all lands believed in Christ. From both peoples God knows his chosen ones. And from both races Christ leads many out of the deep waves of this world to the stability of the future life because the body of water in which Peter and the others fished signifies this present world in which we live, and the shore signifies the stability of the future life, to which Christ leads us if we follow his teaching in our day-to-day lives.

The fishermen who went ashore, leaving that fishing ground to wash their nets, are the teachers who should teach us how to believe in God. And with their nets they draw us out of ignorance and to the holy Savior, who wants us to appropriate into our daily lives the steadfastness of the stable world. The fishermen washed their nets in the water because although teachers should sometimes teach us, at other times they should pay attention to (and instruct and correct) themselves.

"Peter was then a fisherman, who is now an apostle. His ship stood near by then. The Savior climbed into it and commanded Peter to push his ship a little away from the land. And then Christ sat down in the ship near the land and taught the people who stood on the shore, as was his custom." Peter's ship, which stood near there, signified the Jewish people who turned to Christ and believed in him, though some of them chose not to. In them was the beginning of all of the Christian church. The other ship signified the Gentile people from all over the world who with belief acknowledge the dear Savior. And that is the church called *Ecclesia*. The Jewish nation was called *Sinagoga*. That means "gathering" in the English language.

From Peter's ship Christ taught the people on the shore. And the teaching from the land of the Jews came to us through the holy apostles, who taught the Gentiles and converted people of every land to belief. And in God's holy service, Christ's disciples raised churches for the preservation of our Savior's laws, which are still kept inviolate among the good peoples who are mindful of God's will.

But here in the English nation we feebly keep the laws God established to guide and instruct all those who love him. Instead, we create for ourselves new laws entirely different from those God himself taught. These laws are contrary to God's laws and to those of all the wise men who lived before us. With our self-will we rebel against them all. By trampling on God's laws with bad behavior and despising our Lord, as we are doing, we will make the way very difficult for ourselves.

"Then after teaching them, Christ commanded holy Peter to let his ship go out into the deep, and he commanded them to cast out their nets into the fishing ground." Christ taught beside the shore, and then later they took the ship further out, and that symbolizes how Christ himself taught in the land of the Jews but that later his teaching came to all lands, as is well known throughout Christianity.

"Peter answered Christ: 'Dear teacher, we have worked all night, staying awake but without success, and we have caught nothing. But at your word I will now cast out the net.' And then they cast it out." Singing these words about God, the psalmist said, *Nisi Dominus edificauerit domum, in uanum labórant qui aedificant eam*: "Unless the Lord himself builds the house, those who build it work in vain." Unless with his holy grace God himself enlightens the hearts of those who hear God's teaching, the teacher who presents it meets with no success because God's teaching will then remain merely an external notion.

"Then the net immediately filled with fishes and began bursting." And today this is also true. So many people submit along with the chosen ones to Christ's faith in his church, that later some of them break out in an evil manner. And they spend their lives in errors—as the English people do who submit to the Danes—and they are branded by Satan for evil service. And they do the devil's deeds to the destruction of themselves, and they betray their own people to death.

Think about this. Is there anything worse than such a betrayal committed against one's own Lord? No, there is nothing worse because it causes the betrayer to fall into eternal torments, estranged from God and all his saints. Once at the beginning of Christianity some of those who professed to believe in God also behaved like this. When for Christ's faith the holy martyrs were shamefully tortured and killed, then many made their unfaithfulness known by renouncing and forsaking Christ so they might be permitted to live. But later their life was worse than death.

Twice while here on earth the Savior commanded the disciples to fish with a net, and both times their nets immediately filled with fishes, as a great sign. This happened once before and once after Christ's passion. We will first speak about the time before Christ's passion. The disciples' net burst with the catch of fishes because it was a sign, as we said before. And this catch of fishes signifies the holy Church, that is, all Christian people who believe in God now. In it are both the evil and the good, and some of them go astray, as we mentioned.

On the other occasion, after Christ's passion, he commanded them to cast out the net on the right side. And they caught many fishes, some of them very large, and their net did not burst. This was a sign because the catch of fishes after Christ's resurrection certainly signified the happy Christians, who—through God's help—enter, blessed, into the kingdom of God, into eternal life, a place from which none of them can afterwards burst out. And the right hand signified the chosen saints, and that's why the disciples cast the net out on the right hand.

The Gospel we have been discussing today does not say on which side Christ commanded them to cast the net, but the left-hand side does signify the evil ones. However, don't imagine your left hand is evil because both God's teaching and his teachers tell us the righteous person has no left hand. Instead, the hands of the good Christian person are both like right hands.

This Gospel tells us here that "they immediately motioned to their companions on the other ship to come quickly to help them." As we said before, the other ship signifies the Gentile people all over the world who believe in Christ because in the land of the Jews the Savior did not find nearly as many who believed in him as he wanted to give heavenly life. Christ then chose us from all peoples, and in this way he fills the full count he wants to receive his eternal glory.

"Then they came at once and filled both ships with fishes until they almost sank." Christ continues filling the ships until Doomsday, and though they endure much danger and many temptations in this world, God's saints do not sink because Christ himself can protect and always help them.

"When Peter saw such a catch of fish, he immediately fell at the Savior's knees and said to him humbly, awed: 'Depart from me, Lord, for I am a sinful man.'" The Savior did not, however, want to honor Peter's request that he should leave him. Instead, Christ remained with Peter until they reached land, to show that the teachers who teach God's people, bishops and Mass priests, must not succumb to any temptation and abandon God's holy office entrusted to them by God because Christ will rescue them, if for his love they do not abandon his flock.

"Peter was terrified, and so were his companions; and even James and John, the sons of Zebedee, were frightened by that catch of fishes." James and John were brothers, and their father was named Zebedee. And their mother was the sister of Christ's mother, as books tell us.

"Then the Savior spoke these words to holy Peter: 'Don't fear anything because of this event. From now on you will catch men as you caught fishes.'" Because Christ wishes well to all people of good will, the Savior comforted Peter with great kindness, graciously, telling him he would catch men later. And Peter also followed his Lord's words. He did indeed catch many people with his teaching and the wonderful miracles he worked, just as he had caught fishes before with his nets. And we still have his teaching with us in Christian books, and it can help us improve ourselves.

"They rowed their heavy ships to shore, and then they abandoned all things to follow Christ." Christ chose fishermen as his followers. They were unlearned men who rejected all things to follow Christ's teaching and Christ himself here in this world. And later they became so very learned the whole Christian faith in Christ's church was raised up through them, with the help of the Savior.

To him is glory and honor forever. Amen.

Introduction to Sermon XV

Sermon XV was likely written by Ælfric towards the end of his career, sometime during his Eynsham abbacy. Its mature style and freedom in dealing with sources support a late composition date.[1] Sermons XV and XIII may have also been written as a complementary pair.[2] Sermon XV exegetes Matthew 5.20-24 and warns against anger and violence, giving it a natural affinity of theme with the Luke 6.36-42 pericope of sermon XIII and its insistence on God's mercy and human kindness.[3] In both sermons Ælfric develops two subordinate themes: the negative example of hypocrisy on the part of scribes and Pharisees and the positive lawful judgment and admonition by persons in authority.[4]

Ælfric has a particularly Benedictine concern with disciplining the mouth as a first step towards extirpating anger and cultivating kindness. Chapter 6 of *The Rule of St. Benedict* is titled, "On the Spirit of Silence" and is strategically sandwiched between chapter 5, "On Obedience," and chapter 7, "On Humility." In sermon XV, lines 181-87, Ælfric introduces and interprets Psalm 141.3 (Vulgate, 140.3), independently expanding his theme of eschewing anger's violence and embracing gentleness:

> We should bless ourselves and pray God will restrain our mouths and will himself resound through them, as the prophet prayed, saying with these words, *Pone, Domine, custodiam ori meo, et hostium circumstantie labiis meis*: "Dear Lord, place a guard about my mouth, and round about my lips place the door of your protection." He asked for a door, so he could shut out idle words and open his mouth to speak words of wisdom to honor God, just as one closes and opens a door.[5]

The Benedictine mystic nuns, Umiltà of Faenza and St. Gertrude the Great, share this concern with the discipline of silence, highlighting the connection R. W. Chambers describes as existing between Ælfric's prose and the later devotional writers.[6] Umiltà writes in *Sermon 8*:

> My strong Angels, be with me wherever I go and guard me wherever I am. Keep my enemies from my front door. . . . Stand at the first gate with your sword in your right hand. Keep this entrance closed to proud, lazy words.

---

[1]Pope, *Homilies* II.493.
[2]Pope, *Homilies* II.528-29.
[3]Pope, *Homilies* II.528.
[4]Pope, *Homilies* II.529.
[5]Pope, *Homilies* II.530 (XV.181-87).
[6]Chambers, *On the Continuity of English Prose from Alfred to More and His School*, lxi, xc, xciii.

When they want to leave my mouth, don't let them. Sharpen my tongue like a hoe, so it can dig up vices and plant virtues, to the praise and glory of the highest Emperor and his divine Mother.[7]

St. Gertrude uses an extended metaphor in *The Herald of Divine Love* to make the same point: "The Lord asked me to make his feet my hallway, his hands my workshop, his mouth my living room, his eyes my library for sitting and reading, and his ears my confessional."[8]

† † †

---

[7] Butcher, *Incandescence*, June 25.
[8] Butcher, *Incandescence*, May 17.

Sermon XV

For the Seventh Sunday after Pentecost
Matthew 5.20-22

Matthew the Evangelist—who was with Christ in this world and heard his teaching while living in Christ's household—wrote down concerning Christ that on one occasion he spoke these words to his holy apostles and through them also to us: "I tell you the truth, you will not enter the kingdom of heaven unless your righteousness is much greater to my Father than that of the scribes and Pharisees.

"You have heard the commands God gave a long time ago to the Israelites under Moses's law. God said these things to them: 'Don't kill. Anyone who kills a person will be subject to a judge's sentence.' I tell you in truth that whoever is even angry with his own brother will be subject to judgment. Whoever speaks an insult to him will be subject to judgment, and whoever calls his brother a foolish person will be in danger of being punished in the tormenting fire of the world to come, unless during his life he makes amends for that sin. If you offer God any sacrifice at his altar, and then you remember your brother has something against you, set your sacrifice down before the altar, and first go quickly to your own brother and be reconciled to him. And when you come again, offer your sacrifice then."

This Gospel has now been briefly told to you. And we also say to you that some people believed the former law during Moses's time was much harder for people to faithfully observe than Christ's commands, and Christ himself also said this in the new law after his coming under God's grace and during the time of the events narrated by the Gospel. We must faithfully observe these if we serve God. But we learn here in this Gospel that the commands Christ gave people are much greater than Moses's law. And we ought to be gentle. We must in fact turn our lives to the Savior's commands if we want to have great joy in his presence, as he promised us.

There is no way we can live on earth and not sin against God and others in word and deed. But we must always turn to God and ask for his mercy because if we ask him with sincere hearts he is ready to have mercy on us. And the direction of our life is much more important to him than any other gift because he wants us to refuse everything that is evil. We sin every day, and every day we ought to please our Savior with some goodness because he is at every moment willing to have mercy on us people. And Christ never desires the death of a sinner, but he wants that sinner to turn away from sin and live. And anyone who undertakes penance—even if he were to die very soon afterwards—will without a doubt go to the rest of the virtuous after death because he turned from his sins to God.

The Savior said to us, as you heard earlier, "I tell you the truth, you will not enter into the kingdom of heaven unless your righteousness is much greater to my Father than that of the scribes and Pharisees." The scribes and Pharisees were the councilors of old under Moses's law. They were so highly learned that they knew the former law in great detail. However, they didn't keep God's holy law very well. The Savior frequently reprimanded them because they simply did not faithfully observe God's holy commands as God himself commanded. Instead, they imagined they themselves were holy, but they were all wrong internally.

Then the Savior—who saw their hearts—said these awful words of reprimand to them, *Uos iustificatis uos coram hominibus; / Deus, autem, nouit corda uestra*: "You consider yourselves righteous in the sight of men, but God knows your hearts intimately. You are like tombs that on the outside are covered with decorative carvings and fine paint and yet are filled with nothing but rottenness. How you love fame and praise."

Moses's law commanded the scribes and Pharisees to love their friend and hate their enemy. But while he was here in this world, the Savior commanded us to always love our friend and every Christian person without pretense, and also—because of God's love—to love our enemy, so our righteousness would be greater than theirs. Remember, we are destined to enjoy the heavenly life, if we are obedient to God's commands with works.

The scribes and Pharisees were also commanded not to be immoral by having intercourse with other men's wives. But Christ told us this instead: *Omnis qui uiderit mulierem ad concupiscendum eam / iam mechatus est eam in corde suo*. In English that means, "Every man who looks at a woman lustfully, wanting to have intercourse with her, has certainly already performed adultery in his own heart through his evil lust that desired her." We do hasten to add that it is, however, easier to make amends for evil thoughts than for evil deeds, if a person changes the evil desire to something better.

The scribes and Pharisees paid tithes of their herbs and yet wrongly forsook the greater commands Moses gave them to keep according to God's holy law. Now we should keep the lesser commands in such a way that we also fulfill the greater ones with works. As it is written, "They taught God's teaching to men with words but neglected the works." However, the Savior said, "He is the greater teacher who himself first practices and afterwards teaches, first beginning the example in himself."

If they faithfully observed God's old law, earthly fruits were promised them, and everyone who keeps Christ's commands is promised eternal life by Christ. And a person's eye cannot see, nor ear hear, nor heart imagine the great glory the merciful Christ promised to all who love him. And Christ also gives us everything we need. Now that heavenly treasure has been promised us by Christ, we must possess a greater righteousness, so when we leave this life, we will be permitted to journey to Christ immediately, if earlier in life we have prudently and voluntarily made amends for our sins.

"You have heard the commands God gave long ago to the Israelites under Moses's law, saying these things to them: 'Don't kill. Whoever kills a person will be subject to a judge's sentence.' I tell you, however, that whoever is now angry with his own brother will be subject to judgment." At that Judgment the nature of a person's offense is determined, and often someone who previously had been considered guilty will be declared innocent there. And good will can pacify a person's unexpected anger, and also wisdom can arrest it more easily than a person can make amends if he kills someone he is angry with. Lawful judgment is prescribed for both anger and for murder. But a person's penance is lighter if the one he is angry with is still alive. Even if a person is angry, his anger will heal, as the latter part of this Gospel tells us, so we can be reconciled to the person whom we offended earlier.

"Whoever speaks an insult to his brother will be subject to judgment." Here are now two things, anger and insult. And judgment is prescribed for these two things, so by means of deliberation an offender will be sentenced to punishment and will suffer for them both. But sometimes a guilty person escapes, as the interpreter tells us in Latin.

"And whoever calls him a foolish person will be in danger of punishment in the tormenting fire of the world to come." Here are now three things, and therefore greater punishment: anger, insult, and disdain. And as the book tells us, these things must be purified in the future punishment, unless a person voluntarily makes amends for them. Here in this world a person can make amends for much greater sins and can appease the Savior, so he does not need to suffer in the life to come. Through his prophet, God said he will have mercy on every person who turns from his sins to him and does penance with groaning. Afterwards that person's sins will not be in God's memory.

Teachers must instruct and correct, and the wise must reprove the dishonest and the ignorant, both with words and with deeds sometimes, as

Christ himself did. Christ reprimanded the Jews for their errors and contemptuous behavior. Paul the apostle said these words in his epistle, *Argue, obsecra, increpa, in omni patientia et doctrina*: "Rebuke, advise, and reprimand with patience, in keeping with all teaching pertaining to the commandments of Life." If for the purpose of correction anyone now speaks a severe word to his subordinates, reprimanding their foolishness, he is not at all similar to the dissolute person whose lack of consideration leads him to revile another—not for the sake of their guidance—but because of his stupidity.

We should bless ourselves and pray God will restrain our mouths and will himself resound through them, as the prophet prayed, saying with these words, *Pone, Domine, custodiam ori meo, et hostium circumstantie labiis meis*: "Dear Lord, place a guard about my mouth, and round about my lips place the door of your protection." He asked for a door, so he could shut out idle words and open his mouth to speak words of wisdom to honor God, just as one closes and opens a door.

Let us now learn the Savior's remedy. Let us see how here in this world we can heal the evil words we have said against someone we have provoked. "If you offer God any sacrifice at his altar, and then you remember your brother has something against you, set your sacrifice down before the altar, and first go quickly to your brother and be reconciled to him. And when you come again, offer your sacrifice." The Savior said again in another place: "When you stand at your prayers, then forgive in your hearts all the people who have sinned against you, so the heavenly Father may forgive your sins. And unless you forgive, God will not forgive you."

When our brother has something against us, if we injured him or did him wrong, then we must act according to our Lord's teaching and determine to be reconciled to our brother, that Christian person, without pretense, so God himself can gladly receive our gift. Before that reconciliation and before we have peace in a truthful heart, God would have been unwilling to receive anything from us. If any person injures us or wrongs us, we must forgive it, as the Savior said, so our sins can be forgiven us.

Our sacrifices are the holy prayers we offer God and the alms we give to help the poor, and every thing we do as praise to our Lord. These are all God's sacrifices, and we should offer them with good will, so they will be acceptable and pleasing to God, who always loves peace, and always judges all people with gentleness.

Concerning this, the psalmist sang these words to God, *Adiutor meus, tibi sallam, et cetera*. That is in English: "You are my Helper, and I sing to You. You are my Protector, my own true God, and my Mercy." God commanded him to have mercy because God himself is merciful, and in countless ways God helps anyone who with singleness of mind always puts their trust in our Lord.

To whom is glory and honor forever. Amen.

Introduction to Sermon XVI

In sermon XVI, Ælfric exegetes the Parable of the Dishonest Steward (Luke 16.1-9). Few modern pulpiteers treat this difficult parable, but this Anglo-Saxon monk uses two Augustinian sources to teach the practical advantages of almsgiving while at the same time rejecting the steward's deceitfulness.[1] He independently develops his source to distinguish between the good and bad aspects of worldly wisdom, inserting at lines 227ff. the famous admonition of Matthew 10.16: "Be as wise as serpents and as innocent as doves."[2]

Sermon XVI was written sometime after 1005, making it one of Ælfric's maturest works.[3] In another independent development, Ælfric spends a paragraph describing the potentially unknown olive oil, making it more familiar to his audience. Although olive oil was imported into England during the Anglo-Saxon period for both ecclesiastical and cooking purposes, butter, flax, or rape seed oil would most likely have been more commonly known. Ælfric makes sure his audience understands this:

> Oil grows on trees, as does wine, but olive trees are taller, and their fruits larger. And these are gathered and squeezed, and the oil is eaten in many delicacies, just as we eat butter. Olive oil is considered the best of foods. And it is also used to make light throughout the land in beautiful lamps because it is fatty and burns pleasantly inside God's church. Olive oil is very precious, and when it has been sanctified, it is used for baptism and God's other ministries.[4]

☦ ☦ ☦

---

[1] Pope, *Homilies* II.544-45.
[2] Pope, *Homilies* II.556.
[3] Pope, *Homilies* I.148.
[4] Pope, *Homilies* II.552 (XVI.132-41).

Sermon XVI

For the Tenth Sunday after Pentecost
Luke 16.1-9

While here in this world living his life among humanity, the Savior said these words to his holy apostles, for he often spoke to them in parables: "Long ago there was a certain prosperous man who had a steward. Then the steward was brought before his lord and accused of mismanaging and squandering his wealth. And the lord summoned him at once and then asked him: 'What do I hear about you? Resign your office. You can no longer be in my employment.' And the steward then thought to himself: *What will I do now? I will be fired, and yet I can't dig with my feet, nor can I beg anywhere for shame.* And he went on to say to himself, *Before I leave, however, I will make friends among those who owe my lord anything, so they will receive me into their houses when I have resigned from this office.*

"Then he immediately summoned his subordinates to him, those who owed his lord anything in goods, and said to one of them, 'What do you owe as payment?' He said he must pay his lord one hundred casks filled to the proper measure with oil. Then the steward commanded him to write down fifty.

"Then the steward said to another, 'What do you owe your lord?' He said he owed him one hundred measures of wheat. And the steward commanded him to set down in writing that he should pay him eighty. So then later that lord praised this steward because of his unrighteousness, for he had acted wisely towards himself—because the people of this world, this world's children, are much wiser among their generation than the children of Light, who are God's faithful.

"Then the Savior went on to speak these words to them: 'Make friends for yourselves with unrighteous riches, so that when you die they will receive you to them in the eternal dwelling places.' "

The prosperous man who employed that steward is almighty God, who owns all things. And God entrusted his great riches to humanity here in this present life. He gave us understanding and reason, just as he did the angels, above other creatures. And he also gives us what we need in life because he is very generous. He does this because he loves humanity, those who acknowledge him and are friendly to him through true faith and daily love.

Those of us who possess God's riches are his stewards, and we squander God's possessions evilly when we turn our understanding to wickedness and our human reason to cruel sins and when we aren't willing to govern ourselves with reason nor carry out the will of the God who wants to possess us.

And no possession is so dear to God as our souls without taint of sin. The psalmist sang about that, saying these words to us, *Homo, cum in honore esset, non intellexit, et cetera*: "Man was in a position of honor but didn't understand it and instead became equal to the stupid beasts, and then was similar to them." Anyone turning their understanding to acts of evil and away from righteousness refuses to understand their own worth. They refuse to see they are created in God's likeness. And if through foolishness they make themselves unworthy of that great honor, and if they lie instead in the filth of horrible sins, dirtier than beasts, then they have spent their lord's possessions in an evil manner because they have wholly squandered their reason on sins and have made themselves weak and worthless.

These sins displease God: adultery, promiscuity, every kind of robbery, murder, manslaughter, all false oaths, witchcraft, fortune-telling, unjust judgments, stealing, lying, drunkenness, eating at improper times, gluttony, poison-making, and a person's unwillingness to celebrate either the holy Sunday with honor—as praise to the Savior, who himself arose from death on a Sunday, doing many miracles on that day—or his holy Mass days that everyone should faithfully observe by going to church and hearing God's praises.

Let us now repeat or tell you again the beginning of this Gospel text. We told it to you before, but we will repeat it so you can better understand its meaning. "Long ago there was a certain prosperous man who had a steward. Then the steward was brought before his lord and accused of mismanagement and squandering his wealth. And the lord summoned him at once and then asked him: 'What do I hear about you? Resign your office. You can no longer be in my employment.'" The Savior calls us to him in two ways, either in the present life first to penance, or in the other life afterwards to Judgment. Now we ourselves should be careful here in this life to act in such a way that we are not determined to be evil later at the Judgment.

"And the steward then said to himself: *What will I do now? I will be fired, and yet I can't dig with my feet, nor can I beg anywhere for shame.*" We cannot dig in the afterlife, nor can we produce any good fruits then by any action, if we were unwilling to do so before. Nor is there opportunity for reparation in the afterlife, but there will certainly be retribution then for all our deeds, in keeping with what we did before in this life. Nor can we beg for shame there, if we lack every virtue then. Remember the foolish maidens, who had no light in their lamps for the bridegroom, Jesus Christ, as he himself said. And then they wanted to beg or buy light for themselves. But they were shut out from Christ because they had no light in his presence.

The Wisdom of God said about this: "Because of winter's coldness, the sluggard did not want to plough. Then he will beg in the summer and nothing will be given to him." That means anyone who labors little in this life for Christ cannot gain eternal joy later by begging.

"And the steward went on to say to himself, *Before I leave, however, I will make friends among those who owe my lord anything, so they will receive me into their houses when I have resigned from this office.* Then he immediately summoned his subordinates to him, those who owed his lord anything in goods, and said to one of them, 'What do you owe as payment?' He said he must pay his lord one hundred casks filled to the proper measure with oil. Then the steward commanded him to write down fifty."

Oil grows on trees, as does wine, but olive trees are taller, and their fruits larger. And these are gathered and squeezed, and the oil is eaten in many delicacies, just as we eat butter. Olive oil is considered the best of foods. And it is also used to make light throughout the land in beautiful lamps because it is fatty and burns pleasantly inside God's church. Olive oil is very precious, and when it has been sanctified, it is used for baptism and God's other ministries.

"Then the steward said to another, 'What do you owe your lord?' He said he owed him one hundred measures of wheat. And the steward commanded him to set down in writing that he should pay him eighty."

This steward showed mercy to these men so he might hope for their future friendship. He wanted them to invite him into their houses later when he needed it. But we ought to understand this deed more in a spiritual sense. With good deeds of charity we must provide friends for ourselves among God's ministers and God's poor people. Then, after we die we will be permitted to live in the eternal home with the people of God to whom we now give our alms.

We should not make friends for ourselves through fraudulent means, but this story does show us the true model of how we must give alms from lawful gains, as we learn by reading in books. We must distribute alms now and give today before we die, so later we get a return on this investment a hundred times over.

And also no thief can then break in and steal this treasure, nor can moth or rust injure it. Instead it is kept safely stored there for us, safe and sound. Every person must give alms on earth in keeping with their ability. Let the person who has more give more. Let the person who has less give from that little. No person should be without almsgiving.

The Savior said this in another Gospel about giving to the poor: "To your good things call in beggars and cripples, the blind and the lame, and you will be blessed because they have nothing with which they can repay you. Your giving will surely be repaid at the resurrection of the righteous." That is on Doomsday, when we rise up out of death.

Zaccheus the rich was unrighteous at first, but later he received the Chief Guest, who is the Savior himself. Then Zaccheus said, "Dear Lord, I want to distribute my possessions, one half to the poor, and I also want to give quadruply whatever I took unjustly." And then the Savior answered him immediately, "Now today salvation has come to this home," for this almsgiving is how Zaccheus was made righteous by the Savior's coming to his house.

As books tell us, Christ's apostles abandoned their possessions for Christ. Penniless, they followed him wherever he went, and they always possessed heavenly riches. Among those who cast their alms at the holy altar in Jerusalem, there was a certain poor widow who cast one farthing. And immediately the Savior said she had contributed more than anyone else because with a generous heart she had brought all she had to live on, and Christ praised her then.

The Savior also said, "If anyone gives one thirsty person something to drink, even cold water, he will have his reward for that little good deed." Good will is always kind and is therefore acceptable to God, who sees any sacrifice offered to another as being a sacrifice offered to him. We earn the heavenly home by such deeds done as praise to our Lord. They are done without hateful deceit and without fraud, and through such pure good deeds we spiritually fulfill the Gospel word that you heard about here in this reading.

"So then later that lord praised this steward because of his unrighteousness, for he had acted wisely towards himself." Our Lord praises his trustworthy steward with even better praise for performing his Will in the spiritual work of the cultivation of souls. Our Lord praises, saying these words to his faithful steward, *Euge serue bone et fidelis, et reliqua*: "You are a good servant, and splendid in faithfulness to me. You were faithful to me in the little things, so now I will make you ruler over many things. Enter at once into the joy of your lord's good things."

"Yes, the people of this world, this world's children, are much wiser among their generation than the children of Light, who are God's faithful." Worldly people know worldly wisdom and evil, and the Savior abhors their crafty ways. Concerning this, these words are written in books, *Sapientia enim huius mundi stultitia est apud Deum*: "The wisdom of this world is folly before God." You think it very smart that you have what you want and are able to get the better of another person, but Christ wants to have harmlessness in us, and innocence, as he commanded us, *Estote prudentes sicut serpentes, et simplices sicut columbe*: "Be as wise as serpents and as innocent as doves." The serpent is the wisest animal, and through it the devil deceived the first humans.

As the Savior said, we should in this moment be wise against the devil's deceitful ways and look with circumspection on his dishonest tricks, so he cannot lead us off God's path. Every year the serpent discards its old dead skin and is then enveloped by entirely new skin. Let us do this. We must cast off our sins and evil behavior, and learn the good, so we may be inwardly clothed with God's grace. The serpent will also guard its head and coil itself around its head, so that above all, no one can strike the head. We must also do this, if we are wise. Consider nothing dearer than our Savior, who is our Head. And for the sake of Christ's love we should give our bodies over to death, if there is so great a need, before we deny him and lose our soul, the best possession.

And a dove is very innocent, never insolent. A dove loves unity among her companions and is inoffensive and always kind. We should behave like doves. We should be slow to take offense and never bitter with those we love. Then we will not harm them with unrighteous deeds. We must instead have unity in all righteousness, permitting everyone to possess what is rightly theirs. Then we will ourselves possess the innocence the Savior commanded.

"Then the Savior went on to speak these words to them: 'Make friends for yourselves with unrighteous riches, so that when you die they will receive you to them in the eternal dwelling places.'" Unrighteous riches are obviously those worldly material goods in which unrighteous people place their hope and trust, while righteous people convert their material goods and money into their life's needs and live by means of these, but they earnestly place their hope in heavenly riches that are eternal. And those who take from their earthly wealth and short-lived riches of this world and distribute alms to God's servants and God's poor people will later be repaid by God himself. Those who give such alms will have a home in the heavenly kingdom with those with whom they shared and performed good works. Also, teachers who instruct God's people and reform many by means of their examples, can know for certain they will be permitted to live in God almighty's eternal joy because they worked faithfully for their Lord.

The Savior himself said in another place, "The person who is faithful to his lord in a small matter will be faithful to him in the greater ones. And whoever is unfaithful in a lesser matter will be unfaithful in a greater one." This life and its few days are reckoned a small matter in comparison with the eternal world that never ends. And worldly things are surely inferior to spiritual things that are God's own teaching and the holy Wisdom continually drawing us up towards our Creator who created us as humans. Anyone who proves untrue in worldly affairs (by not faithfully distributing heavenly riches) does not prove themselves true to God in spiritual matters. May the Savior make us faithful through the Holy Spirit, so we can do God's Will. To whom be glory forever. Amen.

Introduction to Sermon XVII

Sermon XVII exegetes Mark 7.31-37. It celebrates four miracles of Christ, the one related in the pericope, followed by shorter accounts of three others.[1] Written sometime after Ælfric became abbot in 1005,[2] sermon XVII discusses the recurring positive theme of the Spirit's seven gifts (at lines 121-23)[3] and features much Ælfrician definition: in lines 34-35, this master Benedictine teacher defines *Effeta* as "Be opened," and in lines 21-23 and 80, he defines *Decapolis* as "Ten Towns."[4] Like sermon I, XVII has lacunae from the Cotton fire, indicated in the translation by bracketed asterisks ([* * *]). When possible, these have been completed with intelligent surmises. I relied mainly on Pope's intelligent editorial direction as well as my own experience reading Cotton Vitellius C.v. with a Fiber Optic Light Cord (FOLC).[5] One minor change occurred at line 28, where Pope suggested a lacuna be filled with the following phrase in parentheses: "mid (his halwendum fingr)um" or "with (his holy fingers)," but FOLC showed "mid his halgum handum" or "with his holy hands." Subsequently, the line reads, "And they begged the Savior to touch this man with his holy hands."

---

[1] Pope, *Homilies* II.563.

[2] Pope, *Homilies* I.148.

[3] Pope, *Homilies* II.572 (XVII.121-23); cf. I.297 (V.208-13); I.384-85 (IX.121-49); and I.418 (XI.68).

[4] Pope, *Homilies* II.568 (XVII.34-35); II.568, 570 (XVII.21-23, 80).

[5] See the introduction to sermon I for more information on my use of FOLC; see also Butcher, "Recovering Unique Ælfrician Texts Using the Fiber Optic Light Cord (FOLC)," or online at <http://oenewsletter.org/OEN/index.php?file=essays/index.txt>.

Sermon XVII

For the Twelfth Sunday after Pentecost
Mark 7.31-37

When the Savior was here in this world, he made his home in the land of the Jews, in the city of Nazareth in the Galilean district, but Christ was born in the city of Bethlehem, as books tell. In those days, Christ traveled throughout that district to all synagogues, teaching the people always and proclaiming the Gospel and God's kingdom to humanity. And Christ healed all who were sick, and he drove out every illness and infirmity from everyone who could come to him.

Then Christ's fame spread to the land of Syria and throughout that kingdom. It is a very large country. And the bedridden, the epileptic, the very mad, and those people variously afflicted by many sicknesses were brought to him, and the true Savior healed them all. And many people from everywhere followed Christ then.

The evangelist called Mark, who composed the Gospel belonging to today's Mass, and who was a martyr for Christ, now says to us that "our Savior came to the Galilean Sea, traveling from the limits of the city of the people of Tyre through that of Sidon, into the maritime district of Decapolis, called 'Ten Towns' in books. Then a man who was unable to speak or hear was brought to Christ in the midst of that crowd. And they begged the Savior to touch this man with his holy hands.

"And immediately the Savior led the man from the crowd. Then Christ put his fingers into this man's ears and touched his tongue with healing saliva. Christ looked to heaven and, groaning within with compassion, spoke this one secret word to this man who could not speak or hear: *Effeta*. In our English language, *effeta* means, 'Be opened.' The Lord wanted this man's ears and mouth to open.

"And immediately the ears of this ailing man opened, and his bound tongue also became unbound. And he spoke his own language correctly. Then the Savior commanded those who had brought him not to speak of this miracle to anyone, but they spoke of it all the more with wonder. They told others of Christ's great works, saying these words, 'He has made all things well through his wonderful strength. He made the deaf man hear well, and he made the man who could not speak speak.' "

We have briefly told you this Gospel text in English. Now we want to repeat the same words of this holy Gospel and disclose to you—verse by verse—the spiritual meaning of this holy lore, with its significations. Tyre and Sidon are two cities the Savior once spoke about when he was strongly reprimanding places in which he had worked miracles and signs and yet their residents had not been willing to believe in him or put themselves right, even though they had seen Christ's true miracles and his living signs. God's Son said to the city called Chorazin and to another called Bethsaida: "Shame on you, Chorazin, and shame on you, Bethsaida. If such miracles had been performed in Tyre and Sidon as have been performed in you, long ago they would have done great penance in sackcloth of hair and in ashes. I speak the truth when I say that in some matters there will be less punishment on Doomsday for Tyre and Sidon than there will be for you, who saw my miracles."

The Savior drew near to the coast, to the inconstant waves, which were a sign of the instability of the ignorant people who lived without belief till then. Of these, Christ wanted each one to receive his grace and mercy born in his great generosity. We know Christ came—as that Gospel tells us—to unite the scattered, erratic children of God to his steadfastness [* * *]. He who is our life wanted them all to have life in him and also the [* * *]. A land in the east beyond the river Jordan was then called [* * *], "Decapolis" in books, meaning, "Ten Towns." The Savior came to this area, as this Gospel says, and there through Christ's holy touch he healed the deaf man who could not speak. Christ made him whole, as he did everyone who drew near to him.

This deaf, mute man surely signified all of Adam's descendants, who became extremely deaf through the serpent's words, which were mortal to us in the transgression against God's command, until humanity did not want to hear with belief the holy word of God as guidance. Humanity also grew mute to its Lord's praises after they had spoken with this deceiver and conversed with him with great presumption—because it is evil and poisonous for a person to confer with the wicked devil, as magicians and witches still often do in their sorcery, in order to deceive the unblessed people who resort to them.

The deaf, mute man was not able to ask the holy Savior for his own healing, but his kinsmen who brought him to Christ asked the Lord to heal their brother through his holy power. And Christ kindly granted them this because he is infinitely good and ever compassionate to all right-minded persons who trust in him.

We should also do this, if one of our friends can't themselves seek from the Lord their soul's healing by true confession. Then we must help them. We must pray on their behalf and frequently urge them with God's teaching so they can seek salvation of soul from the Lord and can hear and praise their Creator.

This holy Gospel passage also says, "The Savior immediately led the man away from the crowd" because Christ took him from the tumult of the people so this ailing man could turn him from his earlier bad habits and obediently towards Christ's holy commands. Then this man's good behavior could be pleasing to God as he lived in keeping with God's ways.

"He put His fingers into his ears." The Savior's fingers are healing. They certainly signify the seven graces of the Holy Spirit, who illuminates our hearts. With that same grace, Christ enlightened the mind of the deaf, mute man, so he could hear the healing lore and in this way come to have understanding through the Holy Spirit. And through the Holy Spirit the Savior drove terrible devils from afflicted persons. And Christ himself gave them sanity as honor.

"He touched his tongue with his healing saliva" so that this sick man could speak and also tell others with his human reason about God's mighty works done in him. Every person ought to do that when God enlightens their mind. They must confess their belief to others [* * *].

"Christ looked to heaven, and, groaning inside with compassion, spoke this one secret word to the man who could not speak: *Effeta*. In our English language that means, 'Be opened.'" Christ looked to heaven with a strong grief because in the beginning he himself created us for heavenly things, and it hurt him that we should fall far away from that and into earthly things completely. By Christ's own grieving, he also made it clear that we should desire our heavenly home—for which we were originally created—with grieving hearts and many tears because so great a thing can be merited only by profound desire and a good heart.

Then Christ said *Effeta*—that is, "Be opened." He said, "Be opened," because the deafness that had injured the man up till then and had closed his ears would be undone by Christ's healing touch. On this same note, God's ministers still do this sort of healing when they baptize children. They place their fingers (with their saliva) inside the child's ears and on the child's nose, saying, "*Effeta*." The saliva signifies, as this sermon says, the heavenly Wisdom desiring baptism. And the nose's faculty for smelling signifies the odor apostle Paul wrote this about, *Christi bonus odor sumus Deo in omni loco*: "We ourselves are certainly the aroma of Christ. For God himself we are a good odor in every place." Blessed Job also said: "As long as there is breath still in us, and God's Spirit is in our noses, we are not to speak unrighteousness with our lips, nor contrive falsehoods with our tongues anywhere."

"And immediately the ears of this ailing man opened, and his bound tongue also became unbound. And he spoke his own language correctly." We speak correctly—in right belief—if we believe in the living God and confess him as salvation for ourselves. Now we must be careful after our baptism not to provoke God too greatly through unrighteous words and evil deeds. Instead, we must always please God more and more with mind and mouth, and also with deeds, so our confession is not done in vain.

"Then the Savior commanded those who brought him not to speak of this miracle to anyone, but they spoke of it all the more with wonder. They told others of Christ's great works, saying, 'He has made all things well through his mighty power: He made the deaf hear well, and he made the mute speak.'" The Savior who performed such miracles could have done them so they remained a secret. But Christ commanded these people not to speak of the miracle to anyone because he gave himself to us as an example. He wants us in the good deeds we do for God to always refrain from pride [* * *]. Pride indeed is a capital sin and is very hateful to God, and if we wish to have the heavenly reward, we must therefore separate that evil vice from us because in his holy Gospels the Savior very often forbids this capital sin. Instead, he commands us to do our almsgiving in secret and our prayers inside our locked rooms, so that God himself may repay us for them, for God is the One who sees our secret thoughts.

We want to tell you some of Christ's miracles, for the strengthening of your belief. "Our Lord went aboard a ship, and his disciples followed him. Suddenly a violent storm and roughness came up on the sea, and the ship tossed in the waves. The wind battered them. And the Savior was asleep at the stern. Then Christ's disciples approached him and woke him up, saying: 'Lord, help us. We are going to die!' He answered, 'O you of little faith, why are you frightened?' Then Christ got up and rebuked the wind and the sea, commanding them to be still. And immediately a great tranquility came to the sea, and the oarsmen marveled, saying: 'What sort of man is this, that both winds and sea obey him?'"

The Savior's sleep showed his true humanity, and the miracle his divine majesty. Christ slept as true man, and as almighty Creator Christ then stilled the turbulent sea with one command, he who before had established the boundaries of the sea, so that it might not by any means overrun the earth.

"Then they rowed over the sea and came ashore at the land called the Gadarenes. Just as they went up, a mad man ran towards the Savior. He had a home in the pagan tombs, and no one could bind him with chains or foot-fetters because he easily broke iron chains and completely crushed foot-fetters. He lived on the mountains day and night, and in tombs, raving and beating himself with stones. And no one could walk along that way. He then ran to the Savior when he saw him and fell at Christ's feet, crying with a loud voice, 'You, Savior, Highest Son of God, I beg you not to torture me.' The Savior said to him, 'You unclean spirit, come out of that man.' And then Christ asked him what his name was. The unclean spirit answered through the madman's mouth, saying, 'My name is legion because we are many here.' And then they begged Christ not to drive them out of that area.

"On the side of that hill was a large herd of swine, and the devils asked to be allowed to enter these swine. And because the Savior allowed it, the devils left the man and entered the swine. Then every one of these some two thousand pigs rushed into the sea and drowned there because of the devils' prompting.

"The frightened herdsmen fled to the city to tell others what happened to the swine and the insane man, and the citizens rushed out to the Savior and witnessed the mad man properly clothed and in his right mind. And they knew he had been mad before. Then Christ turned towards the ship, and the insane man asked him to let him go with him. The Lord answered him, 'Go home to your family. Tell them how the Lord did a mighty work in you and how he had mercy on you.' So the man who had been healed left Christ and went about enthusiastically telling others of the Lord's miracles, and people wondered at that."

In books, one legion is said to be six thousand, and this many damned spirits were oppressing that one man until the mild, kindhearted Savior rowed to that land and rescued him. The devils acknowledged our Savior Christ, while the Jewish people rejected Christ foolishly and for that reason are worse than these accursed devils, who fell at the feet of God's Son, overcome by fear. When driven out, the devils would not have dared enter the swine if Christ had not given them permission to do so, nor could they have gone into any person because the almighty Lord had taken our human nature upon himself and would not have permitted it.

The devils chose swine for their black hue and utter filth. If someone who has swinish habits decides to wash themselves from sins by weeping, but afterwards defiles themselves again through sinning, they are just like pigs returning to the dung after being washed—incorrigible animals. Then they will be delivered to terrible devils because of the foul deeds they repeated sinfully. Anyone who often provokes God by sinning and always repeats his evil deeds is like such a pig, and is guilty in God's eyes. We must always praise our Lord for his great miracles, and we must ask mercy for ourselves, and we must reject evil, and we must not repeat it later. Only then can we escape the cruel devils and grow in God through our good behavior.

Finally, we want to tell you of a certain miracle of Christ's, and we will adorn the conclusion with a single interpretation, as Luke wrote it down in the book of Christ, saying these words about our Lord: "The Savior then went to the city of Capernaum in the region of Galilee, where his native land was. And Christ taught them there on the day of rest, and they all wondered at his amazing teaching because his words had great power. And in the synagogue at that time there was a mad man filled with the foul spirit of a devil. And the damned spirit cried out these words then, very vexed: [* * *] 'Christ, [* * *] have you [* * *]. Have you come to destroy and to injure us? Ah! I know for certain you are God's Holy One.' Then the Savior immediately rebuked the devil, saying this to him: 'Be silent at once, and leave this mad man.' And this is how Christ immediately drove that devil from the poor man, in front of them all, and the devil could not injure the man one bit. Then a profound fear entered all of the people, and they felt awe, speaking these words fervently among themselves, 'What indeed is this word, thus miraculous in him, that in authority and power he bids the unclean spirits leave?' Then Christ's fame spread far and wide in every place throughout the earth."

The benevolent Savior worked miracles here in this world to strengthen our faith. He wanted those who saw his miracles to tell of them so we who then hear God's word could know of them when we read what his evangelists recorded about Christ. And we do know he is the Son of the God who created all things and then with his own life delivered us from Satan's power. Because of this, we always give God glory and honor with words and deeds. Amen.

Selected Bibliography

Works Used for the Translations in This Volume

Ælfric. MS Cotton Vitellius C.v. Western Manuscripts Room, British Library, London.
Pope, John C., editor. *Homilies of Ælfric: A Supplementary Collection. Being Twenty-One Full Homilies of His Middle and Later Career for the Most Part Not Previously Edited, with Some Shorter Pieces, Mainly Passages Added to the Second and Third Series.* Two volumes. EETS 259, 260. London: Oxford University Press, 1967, 1968.

Editions of Works by Ælfric

Clemoes, Peter, editor. *Ælfric's Catholic Homilies: The First Series Text.* EETS. Oxford: Oxford University Press, 1997.
Crawford, Samuel J., editor. *The Old English Version of the Heptateuch, Ælfric's Treatise on the Old and New Testament and His Preface to Genesis.* EETS os 160. London: Oxford University Press, 1969.
Eliason, Norman and Peter Clemoes, editors. *Ælfric's First Series of Catholic Homilies. British Museum Royal 7 C. XII fols. 4-218.* EETS. Early English Manuscripts in Facsimile 13. Copenhagen: Rosenkilde and Bagger, 1966.
Elstob, Elizabeth. *An English-Saxon Homily on the Birth-day of St. Gregory: Anciently Used in the English-Saxon Church. Giving an account of the conversion of the English from paganism to Christianity, Translated into Modern English, with Notes, Etc.* London: W. Bowyer, 1709.
_____. *An English-Saxon Homily on the Birth-day of St. Gregory: Anciently Used in the English-Saxon Church. Giving an account of the conversion of the English from paganism to Christianity, Translated into Modern English, with Notes, Etc. London: W. Bowyer, 1709.* Created by Timothy Graham and designed by John Chandler. Kalamazoo MI: The Board of the Medieval Institute, 2002. <http://www.wmich.edu/medieval/research/rawl/elstob/cover.html> (cited 11 October 2004).
Fausbøll, Else, editor. *Fifty-Six Ælfric Fragments: the Newly Found Copenhagen Fragments of Ælfric's Catholic Homilies with Facsimiles.* Copenhagen: University of Copenhagen, 1986.
Fehr, Bernhard, editor. *Die Hirtenbriefe Ælfrics: In Altenglischer und Lateinischer Fassung. 1914.* With a supplement to the introduction by Peter Clemoes. Darmstadt: Wissenschaftliche Buchgesellschaft, 1966.
Garmonsway, G. N., editor. *Colloquy.* Ælfric. Second edition. 1939. Exeter: University of Exeter, 1999.
Godden, Malcolm, editor. *Ælfric's Catholic Homilies: Introduction, Commentary, and Glossary.* EETS. Oxford: Oxford University Press, 2001.
_____. *Ælfric's Catholic Homilies: The Second Series Text.* EETS. London: Oxford University Press, 1979.
Griffiths, Bill, editor. and translator. *St Cuthbert: Ælfric's Life of the Saint in Old English with Modern English Parallel.* Seaham: Anglo-Saxon Books, 1992.

Henel, Heinrich, editor. *Ælfric's De Temporibus Anni*. EETS OS 213. 1942. Woodbridge: Boydell and Brewer, 1970.

Jones, Christopher A. *Ælfric's Letter to the Monks of Eynsham*. Cambridge: Cambridge University Press, 1999.

Needham, G. I., editor. *Ælfric: Lives of Three English Saints*. Seconnd edition. Exeter Medieval English Texts. M. J. Swanton, general editor. Exeter: University of Exeter, 1984.

Skeat, Walter W., editor. *Ælfric's Lives of Saints*. Two volumes. EETS OS 76, 82 and 94, 114. London: N. Trübner & Co., 1881–1885, 1890–1900. Reprinted as 2 volumes, 1966.

Smith, Alexandra. "Ælfric's Life of St. Cuthbert, Catholic Homily II.X: An Edition with Introduction, Notes, Translation, and Glossary." Dissertation, Queen's University at Kingston, 1972.

Temple, Winifred M. "An Edition of the Old English Homilies in the British Museum MS. Cotton Vitellius C.v." Three volumes. Dissertation, Edinburgh University, 1952.

Thorpe, Benjamin, editor and translator. *The Homilies of the Anglo-Saxon Church. The First Part, Containing the Sermones Catholici, or Homilies of Ælfric. In the Original Anglo-Saxon, with an English Version*. Two volumes. Ælfrices Bocgild. London: Richard and John E. Taylor for the Ælfric Society, 1844, 1846.

Whitelock, Dorothy, editor. *Sermo Lupi ad Anglos*. Third edition. Exeter: University of Exeter Press, 1977.

Zupitza, Julius. *Ælfrics Grammatik und Glossar*. Berlin: Weidmannsche Buchhandlung, 1880.

Reference Sources

Old English bibliographies are published annually in two periodicals, *Old English Newsletter* and *Anglo-Saxon England*. *Old English Newsletter* also publishes a comprehensive annual review of Old English scholarship under the title "The Year's Work in Old English Studies." (See below Joseph B. Trahern, Jr. and Peter S. Baker, editors.) The cutting-edge Old English dictionary is now the one being published by the University of Toronto. (See below Antonette diPaolo Healey, editor.) This list is by no means exhaustive.

Biggam, C. P. "Anglo-Saxon Studies: A Select Bibliography." 1989. First HTML (electronic) edition, 1996. Third edition and second HTML edition. Last update, April 1999. <http://bubl.ac.uk/docs/bibliog/biggam/bib03.html> (cited 17 June 2003).

Campbell, Alistair. *An Anglo-Saxon Dictionary Based on the Manuscript Collections of Joseph Bosworth: Enlarged Addenda and Corrigenda*. To the supplement by T. Northcote Toller. Oxford: Clarendon Press, 1972.

DiNapoli, Robert. *An Index of Theme and Image to the Homilies of the Anglo-Saxon Church: Comprising the Homilies of Ælfric, Wulfstan, and the Blickling and Vercelli Codices*. Norfolk: Anglo-Saxon Books, 1995.

diPaolo Healey, Antonette, editor. *The Dictionary of Old English*. Angus Cameron, founding editor. Toronto: Centre for Medieval Studies, University of Toronto, 1986–. <http://www.doe.utoronto.ca/> (cited 24 April 2003).

Greenfield, Stanley B., and Fred C. Robinson. *A Bibliography of Publications on Old English Literature from the Beginnings to the End of 1972*. Toronto: University of Toronto Press, 1980.

Hall, John R. Clark. *A Concise Anglo-Saxon Dictionary*. 1894. Fourth edition, with a Supplement by Herbert D. Meritt. Cambridge: Cambridge University Press, 1960.

Hughes, Andrew. *Medieval Manuscripts for Mass and Office: A Guide to Their Organization and Terminology*. Toronto: University of Toronto Press, 1982.

Ker, N. R. *Catalogue of Manuscripts Containing Anglo-Saxon*. Oxford: Oxford University Press, 1957.

Keynes, Simon. "Anglo-Saxon History: A Select Bibliography." Richard Rawlinson Center for Anglo-Saxon Studies and Manuscript Research, Medieval Institute, Western Michigan University. 1998. Revised and adapted for the web by John Chandler. <http://www.wmich.edu/medieval/rawl/keynes1/> (cited 17 June 2003).

Kleist, Aaron. "An Annotated Bibliography of Ælfrician Studies: 1983–1996." In *Old English Prose: Basic Readings*, edited by Paul E. Szarmach, 503-52. New York: Garland Publishing, 2000.

Latham, R. E., editor. *Dictionary of Medieval Latin from British Sources*. The British Academy. London: Oxford University Press, 1981.

_____. *Revised Medieval Latin Word List from British and Irish Sources*. The British Academy. London: Oxford University Press, 1980.

Leo, Heinrich. *Angelsächsisches Glossar*. Two volumes. Halle: Waisenhauses, 1872.

Niles, John D. "Bibliography of Old English Studies, Briefly Annotated." University of California Berkeley. Updated 21 January 2001. <http://ist-socrates.berkeley.edu/~niles/nilestool2.html> (cited 6 October 2004).

Pulsiano, Phillip. *An Annotated Bibliography of North American Doctoral Dissertations on Old English Language and Literature*. East Lansing MI: Colleagues Press, Inc., 1988.

Reinsma, Luke M. *Ælfric: An Annotated Bibliography*. Garland Reference Library of the Humanities, Volume 617. New York: Garland Publishing, 1987.

Roberts, Jane A., and Christian J. Kay with Lynne Grundy. *A Thesaurus of Old English*. Two volumes. King's College London Medieval Studies 11. London: Centre for Late Antique and Medieval Studies, 1995. Second impression: Two volumes. Costerus n.s. 132. Amsterdam; Atlanta GA: Rodopi, 2000.

Sawyer, P. H. *Anglo-Saxon Charters: An Annotated List and Bibliography*. London: Butler & Tanner, Ltd., 1968.

Scragg, D. G. and Michael Lapidge, editors. *Fontes Anglo-Saxonici: A Database Register of Written Sources used by Authors in Anglo-Saxon England*. Manchester, 1987– . <http://fontes.english.ox.ac.uk/> (cited 4 October 2004).

Szarmach, Paul E., project director. "Anglo-Saxon Bibliography." <http://www.wmich.edu/medieval/saslc/volone/biblio.htm> (cited 24 April 2003).

_____, project director. "Electronic Sources of Anglo-Saxon Literary Culture (SASLC)." <http://www.wmich.edu/medieval/saslc/volone/> (cited 24 April 2003).

Toller, T. Northcote, editor. *An Anglo-Saxon Dictionary Based on the Manuscript Collections of the Late Joseph Bosworth*. Edited and enlarged by T. Northcote Toller. London: Oxford University Press, 1881–1898. Reprint: Oxford; New York: Oxford University Press, 1998.

_____, editor. *An Anglo-Saxon Dictionary Based on the Manuscript Collections of the Late Joseph Bosworth*. Supplement. With revised and enlarged addenda by Alistair Campbell. Oxford: Clarendon Press, 1921. Oxford; New York: Oxford University Press, 1998.

Trahern, Joseph B., Jr., and Peter S. Baker, editors. "The Year's Work in Old English Studies." *Old English Newsletter*. Kalamazoo: Richard Rawlinson Center for Anglo-Saxon Studies and Manuscript Research at the Medieval Institute at Western Michigan University. Appears yearly in the winter issues of *OEN*.

Wanley, Humfrey. "Catalogus Cod. MSS. Anglo-Saxonicorum Bibliothecae Cottonianae, quae est Westmonasterii." In *Humphredi Wanleii Librorum Vett. Septentrionalium, qui in Angliae Bibliothecis extant, nec non multorum Vett. Codd. Septentrionalium alibi extantium Catalogus Historico-Criticus, cum totius Thesauri Linguarum Septentrionalium sex Indicibus*, 183-265. Volume 2 of *Linguarum Vett. Septentrionalium Thesaurus* by George Hickes. Three volumes. Oxford: Sheldonian Theater, 1705.

Wilcox, Jonathan. "Bibliography." In *Ælfric's Prefaces*, edited by Jonathan Wilcox, 87-105. Durham Medieval Texts number 9. Durham: Durham Medieval Texts, 1994.

Wright, Thomas. *Anglo-Saxon and Old English Vocabularies*. Two volumes. Second edition. London: Trübner and Co., 1884.

Wyatt, A. J., and H. H. Johnson. *A Glossary to Ælfric's Homilies*. London: W. B. Clive & Co., 1891.

Primary Sources

Ælfric. MS B.15.34. Trinity College, Cambridge.

_____. MS Cotton Cleopatra B.xiii. British Library, London.

_____. MS Cotton Faustina A.ix. British Library, London.

_____. MS Cotton Vespasian D.xiv. British Library, London.

_____. MSS Hatton 113 and 114. Bodleian Library, Oxford.

_____. MSS 162, 178, 188, 198, 302, and 303. The Parker Library, Corpus Christi College, Cambridge.

Catalogue of the Cotton Manuscripts: Drawn Up between 1631 and 1638. Handwritten in ink. Add. MS 36789. Western Manuscripts Students' Room, British Library, London.

Madden, Sir Frederic. Add. MS 62576. "Madden Repairs to Cotton MSS." Western Manuscripts Students' Room, British Library, London.

_____. Add. MS 62577. "Cottonian MSS—Repairing and Binding Account." Western Manuscripts Students' Room, British Library, London.

_____. Add. MS 62578. "List of the Cottonian Manuscripts Injured or Destroyed in 1731 and their Present State of restoration. 1866." Western Manuscripts Students' Room, British Library, London.

Planta, Joseph. A Catalogue of the Manuscripts in the Cottonian Library, Deposited in the British Museum. MS K.R.4.d. Annotated Copy, in the Keeper's Room of the Western Manuscripts Students' Room of the British Library, London. London: Luke Hansard, 1802.

Smith, Thomas. Catalogus Librorum Manuscriptorum Bibliothecae Cottonianae. Annotated by various hands, in the Keeper's Room of the Western Manuscripts Students' Room of the British Library, London. MS K.R. 4.d. No. 7 (1, 2) in Millar. Oxford: Sheldonian Theater, 1696.

Wanley, Humfrey. Handwritten Additions Made in Smith's 1696 Catalogue: These Include a MS Copy of the 22 June 1703 Report of the Commissioners (Matthew Hutton, John Anstis, and Humfrey Wanley), Notes of the Number of ff. of Each Cotton MS, and a MS Copy of Wanley's Catalogue of the Cotton Charters. Add. MS 46911. No. 7 (3) in Millar. Western Manuscripts Students' Room, British Library, London.

Secondary Sources

Adriaen, Marci., editor. *S. Gregorii Magni Moralia in Iob*. Corpus Christianorum Latina Series. Three volumes. Turnhout: Brepols, 1979–1985.

Algeo, John. Notes to the author. January 1991.

_____. "The Forty Soldiers: An Edition." Ph.D. disseretation, University of Florida, 1960.

Amos, Thomas L. "Monks and Pastoral Care in the Early Middle Ages." In *Religion, Culture, and Society in the Early Middle Ages*, edited by Thomas F. X. Noble and John J. Contreni, 165-80. SMC XXIII. Kalamazoo: Medieval Institute Publications, 1987.

Assmann, Bruno, editor. *Angelsächsische Homilien und Heiligenleben. Bibliothek der Angelsächsischen Prosa 3*. Kassel: Georg H. Wigand, 1889.

Baasten, Matthew. *Pride according to Gregory the Great: A Study of the Moralia*. Studies in the Bible and Early Christianity, volume 7. Lewiston NY: Edwin Mellen Press, 1986.

Barry, Patrick, O.S.B. *Saint Benedict's Rule: A New Translation for Today*. Herefordshire: Ampleforth Abbey Press, 1997.

Ben-Sasson, H. H., editor. *A History of the Jewish People*. London: Weidenfeld and Nicolson, 1977.

Bernstein, Melissa J., editor. *The Electronic Sermo Lupi Ad Anglos*. New York: University of Rochester. <http://www.cif.rochester.edu/%7Emjbernst/wulfstan/sermo_index.html> (cited 9 September 2004).

Berry, Mary. "What the Saxon Monks Sang: Music in Winchester in the Late Tenth Century." In *Bishop Æthelwold: His Career and Influence*, edited by Barbara Yorke, 149-60. Woodbridge: Boydell Press, 1997.

Bethurum, Dorothy. *The Homilies of Wulfstan*. Oxford: Clarendon Press, 1957.

_____. "Wulfstan." In *Continuations and Beginnings: Studies in Old English Literature*, edited by Eric G. Stanley, 210-46. London: Thomas Nelson and Sons, Ltd., 1966.

Bhattacharji, Santha, translator. *Reading the Gospels with Gregory the Great: Homilies on the Gospels, 21-26*. Petersham MA: St. Bede's Publications, 2001.

Biblia Sacra Iuxta Vulgatam Versionem. Second edition. Tomus I: Genesis-Psalmi. Stuttgart: Württembergische Bibelanstalt, 1975.

Boenig, Robert, translated and introduced by. *Anglo-Saxon Spirituality: Selected Writings*. Classics of Western Spirituality. New York: Paulist Press, 2000.

Butcher, Carmen Acevedo. "The Feminine Nature of Ælfric's Works." In *Magistra: A Journal of Women's Spirituality in History* (edited by Sister Judith Sutera and Brother John Crean) (December 2003).

———. "Recovering Unique Ælfrician Texts Using the Fiber Optic Light Cord (FOLC)," *Old English Newsletter* (edited by Roy M. Liuzza) 36/3 (December 2003). The Board of the Medieval Institute, Western Michigan University. <http://oenewsletter.org/OEN/index.php?file=essays/index.txt> (cited 4 October 2004).

———. *Incandescence: 365 Readings with Women Mystics.* Orleans MA: Paraclete Press, 2005.

Chambers, R. W. *On the Continuity of English Prose from Alfred to More and His School.* EETS OS 186a. 1932. London: Oxford University Press, 1950.

Chittister, Joan. *Wisdom Distilled from the Daily: Living the Rule of St. Benedict Today.* San Francisco: HarperSanFrancisco, 1991.

———. *The Rule of Benedict: Insight for the Ages.* New York: Crossroad Publishing Company, 1992.

Clark, Mary T., translated and introduced by. *Augustine of Hippo: Selected Writings.* New York: Paulist Press, 1984.

Clark, Willene B. and Meradith T. McMunn, eds. *Beasts and Birds of the Middle Ages: The Bestiary and Its Legacy.* Philadelphia: University of Pennsylvania Press, 1989.

Clemoes, Peter. "Ælfric." In *Continuations and Beginnings: Studies in Old English Literature*, edited by Eric Gerald Stanley, 176-209. London: Thomas Nelson and Sons, Ltd., 1966.

———. "The Chronology of Ælfric's Works." In *The Anglo-Saxons*, edited by Peter Clemoes, 212-47. London: Bowes and Bowes, 1959.

———. "The Chronology of Ælfric's Works." In *Old English Prose: Basic Readings*, edited by Paul E. Szarmach, 29-72. New York: Garland Publishing, 2000.

Davis, Henry, translator. *St. Gregory the Great Pastoral Care.* New York: Newman Press, 1950.

Dietrich, Edward. "Abt Ælfrik: zur Literatur-Geschichte der angelsächsischen Kirche." In *Zeitschrift für die Historische Theologie* (edited by C. W. Niedner, Wittenbeg) 25 (1855): 487-594, and 26 (1856): 163-256.

Dix, Dom Gregory. *The Shape of the Liturgy.* Second edition. Westminster: Dacre Press, 1945.

Doyle, Leonard, trans. *The Rule of St. Benedict.* Collegeville MN.: Liturgical Press, 2001.

de Dreuille, Mayeul, O.S.B. *The Rule of Saint Benedict: A Commentary in Light of World Ascetic Traditions.* New York: Paulist Press, 2002.

Evans, G. R. *The Thought of Gregory the Great.* Cambridge: Cambridge University Press, 1986.

Frantzen, Allen J. *The Literature of Penance in Anglo- Saxon England.* New Brunswick: Rutgers University Press, 1983.

Fry, Timothy, O.S.B., editor. *RB1980: The Rule of St. Benedict in English: In Latin and English with Notes.* Collegeville MN: Liturgical Press, 1981.

Garmonsway, G. N., editor. *The Anglo-Saxon Chronicle.* Second edition, 1953. London: J. M. Dent & Sons, Ltd., 1972.

Gatch, Milton McC. "The Achievement of Ælfric and His Colleagues in European Perspective." In *The Old English Homily and Its Backgrounds*, edited by Paul E. Szarmach and B. F. Huppé, 43-73. Albany: State University of New York Press, 1978.

_____. "The Office in Late Anglo-Saxon Monasticism." In *Learning and Literature in Anglo-Saxon England*, edited by Michael Lapidge and Helmut Gneuss, 341-62. Cambridge: Cambridge University Press, 1985.

_____. *Preaching and Theology in Anglo-Saxon England: Ælfric and Wulfstan*. Toronto: University of Toronto Press, 1977.

Gildea, Joseph, O.S.A., translator. *Source Book of Self-Discipline: A Synthesis of Moralia in Job by Gregory the Great*. New York: Peter Lang, 1991.

Godden, Malcolm. "Ælfric and the vernacular prose tradition." In *The Old English Homily and its Background*, edited by Paul E. Szarmach and B. F. Huppé, 99-117. Albany: State University of New York Press, 1978.

_____. "Anglo-Saxons on the Mind." In *Learning and Literature in Anglo-Saxon England*, edited by Michael Lapidge and Helmut Gneuss, 271-98. Cambridge: Cambridge University Press, 1985.

_____. "The Sources of *Catholic Homilies*, C.B.1.2.6.005.02 and C.B.1.2.45.013.02," 1997, 1988. *Fontes Anglo-Saxonici: World Wide Web Register*. Edited by D. G. Scragg and Michael Lapidge. Manchester, 1987– . <http://fontes.english.ox.ac.uk/> (cited 29 September 2004).

Godfrey, John. *The Church in Anglo-Saxon England*. Cambridge: Cambridge University Press, 1962.

Goppelt, Leonhard. *Typos: The Typological Interpretation of the Old Testament in the New*. Translated by Donald H. Madvig. Grand Rapids MI: William B. Eerdmans Publishing Co., 1982.

Green, Eugene A. "Ælfric the Catechist." In *De Ore Domini: Preacher and Word in the Middle Ages*, edited by Thomas L. Amos, Eugene A. Green, and Beverly Mayne Kienzle, 61-74. SMC XXVII. Kalamazoo: Medieval Institute Publications, 1989.

Greenfield, Stanley B. *A Critical History of Old English Literature*. New York: New York University Press, 1965.

_____, and Daniel G. Calder. *A New Critical History of Old English Literature*. New York: New York University Press, 1986.

Gretsch, Mechthild. "The Benedictine Rule in Old English." In *Words, Texts, and Manuscripts*, edited by Michael Korhammer, 131-58. Woodbridge: D. S. Brewer, 1992.

_____. *Die Regula Sancti Benedicti in England und Ihre Altenglische Übersetzung*. Munich: Wilhelm Fink, 1973.

_____. *The Intellectual Foundations of the English Benedictine Reform*. Cambridge Studies in Anglo-Saxon England 25. Cambridge: Cambridge University Press, 1999.

Grundy, Lynne. *Books and Grace: Ælfric's Theology*. King's College London Medieval Studies VI. London: King's College, 1991.

_____. "þurh boclice lare getrymmed: The Augustinian Teaching of Ælfric of Eynsham." Dissertation, King's College London, University of London, 1989.

Halvorson, Nelius O. "Doctrinal Terms in Ælfric's Homilies." In *University of Iowa Humanistic Studies* 5/1, edited by Franklin H. Potter, 3-98. Iowa City: University of Iowa, 1938. Originally released 1932.

Hamilton, Sarah. *The Practice of Penance, 900–1050*. Royal Historical Society Studies in History. Woodbridge: Boydell & Brewer, 2001.

Hardy, A., A. Dodd, and G. D. Keevil, eds. *Ælfric's Abbey: Excavations at Eynsham Abbey, Oxfordshire, 1989–1992*. Thames Valley Landscapes Monograph 15. Oxford: Oxbow Books Limited, 2002.

Harmer, F. E. *Anglo-Saxon Writs*. Manchester: Manchester University Press, 1952.

Harris, Stephen J. *Race and Ethnicity in Anglo-Saxon Literature*. New York: Routledge, 2003.

Hill, David. *An Atlas of Anglo-Saxon England*. Oxford: Basil Blackwell Publisher, 1981.

Hill, Edmund, editor and translator. *The Works of St. Augustine: A Translation for the Twenty-First Century*. Augustinian Heritage Institute. Twenty-four volumes. John E. Rotelle, general editor. New York: New York City Press, 1992–1998.

Hill, Joyce. "Ælfric's Use of Etymologies." In *Old English Prose: Basic Readings*, edited by Paul E. Szarmach, 311-25. New York: Garland Publishing, 2000.

Holmes, T. Rice. *Ancient Britain and the Invasions of Julius Caesar*. London: Humphrey Milford, 1936.

Hulme, William H., editor. *The Middle-English Harrowing of Hell and Gospel of Nicodemus*. EETS Extra Series 100 (c). London: Kegan Paul, Trench, Trübner & Co., Ltd., 1907.

Hurt, James. *Ælfric*. New York: Twayne Publishers, Inc., 1972.

John, Eric. "The Age of Edgar." In *The Anglo-Saxons*, edited by James Campbell, 160-91. Ithaca: Cornell University Press, 1982.

———. "The World of Abbot Ælfric." In *Ideal and Reality in Frankish and Anglo-Saxon Society*, edited by Patrick Wormald with Donald Bullough and Roger Collins, 300-16. Oxford: Basil Blackwell, 1983.

Jungmann, J. A. *The Mass of the Roman Rite: Its Origins and Development (Missarum Sollemnia)*. Translated by Rev. Francis A. Brunner. Two volumes. New York: Benziger Bros., Inc., 1950.

———. *Pastoral Liturgy*. London: Challoner Publications, 1962.

Kardong, Terrence G. *Benedict's Rule: A Translation and Commentary*. Collegeville MN: Liturgical Press, 1996.

Ker, N. R. *Medieval Libraries of Great Britain: A List of Surviving Books*. Second edition. Offices of the Royal Historical Society. London: Butler & Tanner, Ltd., 1964.

Knowles, David M. *Bare Ruined Choirs: The Dissolution of the English Monasteries*. Cambridge: Cambridge University Press, 1976.

———. *The Monastic Order in England*. Second edition. Cambridge: Cambridge University Press, 1963.

———, and Neville Hadcock. *Medieval Religious Houses: England and Wales*. London: Longman Group, Ltd., 1971.

Lapidge, Michael. "Æthelwold as Scholar and Teacher." In *Bishop Æthelwold: His Career and Influence*, edited by Barbara Yorke, 89-117. Woodbridge: Boydell Press, 1997.

Legg, Rodney. *Cerne's Giant and Village Guide*. Sherborne: Dorset Publishing Co., 1986.

Leinenweber, John, translator. *Pastoral Practice: Books 3 and 4 of the Regula Pastoralis*. Harrisburg PA: Trinity Press International, 1998.

Liuzza, Roy M., editor. *The Old English Version of the Gospels*. Two volumes. EETS os 304, 314. Oxford: Oxford University Press, 1994, 2000.

_____, with A. N. Doane, editors. *Anglo-Saxon Manuscripts in Microfiche Facsimile*, Volume 6: *Gospels*. Binghamton NY: Medieval and Renaissance Texts and Studies, 1995.
Logeman, H., editor. *Saint Benedict of Nursia. The Rule of S. Benet: Latin and Anglo-Saxon Interlinear Version*. London 1888. N.p.: Elibron Classics Series, 2003.
Markus, R. A. *Gregory the Great and His World*. Cambridge: Cambridge University Press, 1997.
Matthew, Donald. *Atlas of Medieval Europe*. Oxford: Phaidon Press Ltd., 1986.
May, Herbert G., and Bruce M. Metzger, editors. *The New Oxford Annotated Bible with the Apocrypha*. Revised Standard Version. New York: Oxford University Press, 1973, 1977.
Mayr-Harting, Henry. *The Coming of Christianity to Anglo-Saxon England*. Third edition. University Park: Pennsylvania State University Press, 1991.
McGinn, Bernard. *Antichrist: Two Thousand Years of the Human Fascination with Evil*. San Francisco: HarperSanFrancisco, 1994.
_____. "The End of the World and the Beginning of Christendom." In *Apocalypse Theory and the Ends of the World*, edited by Malcolm Bull, 58-89. Oxford: Blackwell, 1995.
McGowan, Joseph P. "An Introduction to the Corpus of Anglo-Latin Literature." In *A Companion to Anglo-Saxon Literature*, edited by Phillip Pulsiano and Elaine Treharne, 11-49. Oxford: Blackwell Publishers, 2001.
Morris, R., editor. *The Blickling Homilies of the Tenth Century*. 1874–1880. EETS OS 58. Woodbridge: Boydell & Brewer, 1997.
The New English Bible with the Apocrypha. New York: Cambridge University Press, 1971.
Nichols, Ann Eljenholm. "Methodical Abbreviation: A Study in Ælfric's Friday Homilies for Lent." In *The Old English Homily and Its Backgrounds*, edited by Paul E. Szarmach and B. F. Huppé, 157-80. Albany: State University of New York Press, 1978.
Order of St. Benedict. *The Rule of St. Benedict: An Index to Texts On-Line and Gateway to RB Bibliographic Index*. Collegeville MN: St. John's Abbey. <http://www.osb.org/rb/index.html#English> (cited 17 June 2004).
Payne, Ann. *Medieval Beasts*. London: The British Library, 1990.
Petersen, Joan M. *The Dialogues of Gregory the Great in Their Late Antique Cultural Background*. Toronto: Pontifical Institute of Mediaeval Studies, 1984.
Powell, Kathryn, and Donald Scragg, editors. *Apocryphal Texts and Traditions in Anglo-Saxon England*. Woodbridge: Boydell & Brewer, 2003.
Quennell, Marjorie, and C. H. B. *Everyday Life in Roman and Anglo-Saxon Times, Including Viking and Norman Times*. 1959. New York: Dorset Press, 1987.
Quinn, Karen J., and Kenneth P., editors. *A Manual of Old English Prose*. Garland Reference Library for the Humanities 453. New York and London: Garland Publishing, 1990.
Robertson, A. J. *Anglo-Saxon Charters*. Cambridge: Cambridge University Press, 1939.
Rumble, Alexander R., and A. D. Mills, editors. *Names, Places, and People. An Onomastic Miscellany in Memory of John McNeal Dodgson*. Stamford: Paul Watkins, 1997.
Salter, H. E., editor. *Eynsham Cartulary*. Two volumes. Oxford Historical Society 49, 51. Oxford: Clarendon Press, 1907, 1908.

Sisam, Kenneth. "MSS Bodley 340 and 342: Ælfric's Catholic Homilies." In *Studies in the History of Old English Literature*, 148-98. Oxford: Clarendon Press, 1988.

Skinner, Patricia, editor. *Jews in Medieval Britain: Historical, Literary, and Archaeological Perspectives*. Woodbridge: Boydell & Brewer, 2003.

Smalley, Beryl. *The Study of the Bible in the Middle Ages*. Third edition. 1952. Oxford: Basil Blackwell, 1983.

Stafford, P. A. "Church and Society in the Age of Ælfric." In *The Old English Homily and Its Background*, edited by Paul E. Szarmach and B. F. Huppé, 11-42. Albany: State University of New York Press, 1978.

Stanton, Robert. *The Culture of Translation in Anglo-Saxon England*. Cambridge: D. S. Brewer, 2002.

von Steiger, Christoph and Otto Homburger, eds. *Physiologus Bernensis. Facsimile of the Codex Bongarsianus 318 in Berne's Burger Library*. Basel: Alkuin-Verlag, 1964.

Stenton, Sir Frank Merry. *Anglo-Saxon England*. 1943. Third edition. Oxford: Oxford University Press, 1971.

Sweet, Henry, editor. *Alfred's West-Saxon Version of Gregory's Pastoral Care*. EETS 45, 50. London: N. Trübner & Co., 1871.

Symons, Dom Thomas, editor and translator. *Regularis Concordia Anglicae Nationis Monachorum Sanctimonialiumque: The Monastic Agreement of the Monks and Nuns of the English Nation*. London: Thomas Nelson and Sons, 1953.

Szarmach, Paul E. "Ælfric Revises: The Lives of Martin and the Idea of the Author." In *Unlocking the Wordhord: Anglo-Saxon Studies in Memory of Edward B. Irving, Jr.*, edited by Mark C. Amodio and Katherine O'Brien O'Keefe, 38-61. Toronto: University of Toronto Press, 2003.

————, editor. *Old English Prose: Basic Readings*. New York: Garland Publishing, 2000.

de Waal, Esther, and Kathleen Norris. *Seeking God: The Way of St. Benedict*. Second edition, Collegeville MN: Liturgical Press, 2001.

Walsh, Katherine, and Diana Wood, editors. *The Bible in the Medieval World: Essays in Memory of Beryl Smalley*. Ecclesiastical History Society Series 4. Oxford: Blackwell, 1985.

Weber, R. *Biblia Sacra Iuxta Vulgatam Versionem (104209)*. New York: American Bible Society, 1990.

White, Caroline L. *Ælfric: A New Study of His Life and Writings: With a Supplementary Classified Bibliography Prepared by Malcolm R. Godden*. Yale Studies in English 2. 1898. Edited by Albert S. Cook. Hamden: Archon Books, 1974.

Whitelock, Dorothy. "The Anglo-Saxon Achievement." In *History, Law and Literature in 10th-11th Century England*, 13-43. Collected Studies Series 128. London: Variorum Reprints, 1981.

————. "Two Notes on Ælfric and Wulfstan." 1943. In *History, Law, and Literature in 10th–11th Century England*, 122-26. London: Variorum Reprints, 1981.

Wilcox, Jonathan, editor. *Ælfric's Prefaces*. Durham Medieval Texts 9. Durham: Durham Medieval Texts, 1994.

————. "Transmission of Literature and Learning: Anglo-Saxon Scribal Culture." In *A Companion to Anglo-Saxon Literature*, edited by Phillip Pulsiano and Elaine Treharne, 50-70. Oxford: Blackwell Publishers, 2001.

Woollcombe, K. J. "The Biblical Origins and Patristic Development of Typology." In *Essays on Typology*, 39-75. London: SCM Press, 1978.
Wrenn, C. L. "Some Aspects of Anglo-Saxon Theology." In *Studies in Language, Literature, and Culture of the Middle Ages and Later*, edited by E. Bagby Atwood and Archibald A. Hill, 182-89. Austin: University of Texas Press, 1969.
⎯⎯⎯⎯. *A Study of Old English Literature*. London: George G. Harrap & Co., 1967.
Yorke, Barbara, editor. "Introduction." In *Bishop Æthelwold: His Career and Influence*, edited by Barbara Yorke, 1-12. Woodbridge: The Boydell Press, 1997.